The

Rancho La Puerta

Cookbook

Bill Wavrin

foreword by Deborah Szekely

The

Rancho La Puerta

Cookbook

175 Bold Vegetarian

Recipes from America's

Premier Fitness Spa

BROADWAY BOOKS

NEW YORK

BROADWAY

Broadway Books titles may be purchased for business or promotional use or for special sales. For information, please write to: Special Markets Department, Bantam Doubleday Dell Publishing Group, Inc., 1540 Broadway, New York, NY 10036.

BROADWAY BOOKS and its logo, a letter B bisected on the diagonal, are trademarks of Broadway Books, a division of Bantam Doubleday Dell Publishing Group, Inc.

Library of Congress Cataloging-in-Publication Data
Wavrin, Bill.
    The Rancho La Puerta cookbook: 175 bold vegetarian recipes from America's premier fitness spa / Bill Wavrin; foreword by Deborah Szekely. — 1st ed.
        p.   cm.
    Includes index.
    ISBN 0-7679-0163-0 (paper)
    1. Vegetarian cookery.   2. Rancho La Puerta (Mexico)   I. Title.
TX837.W38   1998
641.5′636—dc21
97-51384

CIP

FIRST EDITION

Designed by Pei Loi Koay

00   01   02   10   9   8   7   6   5   4

This book is dedicated to

Hank, Jeanne, Rosie, Jonathon, and Cheri

and my Mexican family—

the compañeros *I work*

and live with every day.

Contents

Foreword

OVER THE PAST HALF CENTURY, *many chefs have shared their talents with us at Rancho La Puerta, but Bill Wavrin has a special place in my heart. Fun-loving Bill is the big, outgoing man with a hearty laugh who's been known to wear the loudest-colored pants of any chef in the Western Hemisphere.*

Bill, the consummate professional, brings a consistency and quality to food at the Ranch that echoes his passion and commitment to everything he does.

And Bill, the experimenter, never rests: I love his search for new flavors and piquancy. His many new recipes each year bring an unmatched breadth to our vegetarian cuisine.

Our spa cuisine celebrates its origins here in Baja California, Mexico. I first came to this valley in Tecate, at the base of Mt. Kuchumaa, on June 6, 1940, with my husband Edmond Szekely, "The Professor," a Hungarian scholar, philosopher, and natural living experimenter. We founded the Ranch that same summer, asking guests to bring their own tents! Today I still press oil from the olive trees we planted in those early years. Our organic gardens, watered by deep, pure well water, thrive in the soil's abundance—as they have from the beginning.

Guests thrive as well, feeling Kuchumaa's remarkable natural presence and power. In only a week they learn that the body has an incredible ability to respond to kindnesses—not the least of which are rest, stretching, vigorous activity, and eating well. Be kind to your body and like a person it smiles back. Don't tell it what to do. Do you instruct blood to clot as soon as you scratch your hand on a thorn when gardening? Of course not; it happens automatically, a small drama in the body's infinite wisdom of response and regeneration. The same can be true for mind, body, and spiritual health.

Because we are all pioneers in the exploration of longer life spans, I ask you now more than ever to consider the possible cumulative effect of chemicals, pesticides, and certain animal products on your body. You deserve lifelong vitality and health, and it can begin with two simple questions:

Is it life enhancing? Or is it life diminishing?

Bill's recipes are the culinary treasure-house of creativity and vitality you've been searching for.

I'm as delighted by this cookbook's sense of good humor and casual companionship as I am by its breadth of recipes and practical advice. Like an old friend, it takes me back to many memories of years spent here at the Ranch with my family. Today my children, Alex and Sarah Livia, and our dear friend, José Manuel Jasso, carry on the spirit of the professor's favorite motto, Siempre mejor—Always better!

From the moment we set foot here we knew that the land and its bounty would provide us with the joyous energy we needed. Please, join us at our table. Eat well! Be well!

—Deborah Szekely
Founder

Acknowledgments

MUCHAS GRACIAS, MIS AMIGOS Y AMIGAS, TO:

Deborah Szekely, Rancho La Puerta's founder, who helped me understand my newfound cuisine and its wiser—and delicious—avenues toward living a healthier life. Deborah, with her passion for excellence and nonstop energy, inspires me in all that I do.

Alex Szekely, the Ranch's president, who from my first day here in 1988 has stood beside me with his support, insight, honesty, altruism, and deep knowledge of health, all given with open friendship. Two years ago Alex asked me to start compiling this cookbook. Siempre mejor, Alex!

Sarah Livia Szekely Brightwood, architect of the Ranch's incredible landscaping and gardens, who allowed me to experience a chef's dream first-hand. I live at Tres Estrellas, Rancho La Puerta's six-acre organic garden at the base of Mt. Kuchumaa, only steps from the rows and orchards where our kitchen's fresh fruits and vegetables are picked every day. Sarah Livia's spiritual insight into the purity of nature and the wholesome organic food we grow has changed my cooking forever.

José Manuel Jasso, managing partner, whose vision and wisdom over the past 38 years has guided the Ranch staff and the Ranch to all it is today.

Rebecca Kissler, my culinary friend and fellow professional, who tested and retested recipes with patience and great skill.

Michel Stroot, the executive chef at the Golden Door, our sister spa, my friend and fellow chef, who helped me gain a better understanding of spa cuisine as we've worked side by side on occasion, both at the Ranch and at the Door. Merci, Michel, je vous remercie beaucoup!

All my colleagues in the Ranch kitchen, especially sous chefs Rigoberto Ramirez and Gonzalo Mendoza, first cooks Chano Pacheco and Jesus Tapia, and Salvador Pacheco, Christina Cervantez, Gabriel Calderon, Louis Fernando Salas, Aurora Ramirez, Horacio Valle, Luis Garcia, and Manuel Esquier; outside of the kitchen, the special help of Miguel Castro and Miguel Garambullo is especially appreciated.

Maitre d' Martin Cortiso, assistant Maitre d' Jesus Garcia, and all of the waitstaff "out front," who befriend every guest.

Our hard-working gardeners, all seven, under the direction of Enrique Ceballos. Without them, how would any meal—or this cookbook—have seen the finish line?

Peter Jensen and Anne Bernstein assisted me with deadlines as did the director of communications for Rancho La Puerta and the Golden Door, Mary-Elizabeth Gifford.

Harriet Bell, my editor, and Mary Goodbody, whose vision, sensitivity, and skill are what bring the spirit of the Ranch to the printed page and the home kitchen.

My dear wife, Rosie, and my beautiful children, Jonathon and Cheri, who helped me with many culinary creations in our home, even when it came time to clean up. They've eaten everything in the book, twice.

Finally, my great thanks to the 150 Ranch guests of each and every week—and the many thousands who return over the years: their arrival is both a joyous family reunion and a chance to make new friends. Few chefs have the opportunity to test their culinary talents before a more cosmopolitan and well-rounded (sorry, wrong word) gathering. I am a very lucky and grateful man.

Introduction

IT'S DARK NOW OUTSIDE *my little adobe house in Mexico at the base of Mt. Kuchumaa. The wife and kids are asleep. Once again the night sky is the same clear, star-strewn blanket that greeted the ancients when they came to Kuchumaa, their holy place. The crickets are cricking and the frogs are croaking down in the little streambed next to my one-lane dirt road. Here I am at my desk again, hunting and pecking late into the night, a chef who is more comfortable holding knives and ladles than searching for letters on this keyboard.*

Scents come to me through the open window, scents carried by the cool air sliding off the mountain and crossing Rancho La Puerta's organic gardens and orchards. I live in the middle of many acres of lavender, rosemary, and sage and ribbons of mixed flowers that bind up the edges of a freshly planted vegetable garden in Baja California called Rancho Tres Estrellas (Three Star Ranch).

In May the temperatures at our 1,500 feet of elevation are ideal for encouraging the new plantings of fennel, green onions, peppers, lettuces, herbs, carrots, broccoli, cabbages, cauliflower, garlic, leeks, chard, radicchio, radishes, turnips, and more. Come morning, when I walk the rows before going to the spa's main kitchen, I'll see asparagus spears almost jumping toward the sun, begging to be snipped.

Nearby, a little house by the garden gate holds the Ranch's breakfast kitchen. Jasmine and roses cover its buff-colored walls and climb into the tiled ends of shady eaves. Yonder is a wooden bridge that leads to a greenhouse. Inside is a multitude of seedlings, all of my choosing.

All I can think is "Wow!" I live in a chef's dream world. I have been here for over six years. This is my home in the despacio *world of Old*

Mexico with its fantastic culture, traditions, and friendly people, yet I can also look toward Kuchumaa's grand crest and say hello to the good ol' U.S. of A. Within a shout of my backyard is the California border running right across the mountaintop.

Do I have the best of both worlds? You bet. Every night I give a silent thank-you.

This is where the bountiful produce grows that we serve at Rancho La Puerta, the spa that originated the modern fitness resort concept. I never forget that Deborah and her late husband Edmond Szekely, "The Professor," first came here in 1940, established its traditions of eating healthy, and began sharing their secrets of healthy living. My recipes spring from these two great original thinkers, as well as their son Alex and daughter Sarah Livia. The Ranch's general manager, Sr. Jasso (José Manuel Jasso Peña), with the Ranch for over 38 years, is also a great mentor.

I feel as if I've become part of their family, as do all who work here. They keep me challenged, along with 150 different guests each week from all over the world. Some of these worldly spa-goers may have dined under three Michelin stars in France or the trendiest spot in New York, Los Angeles, or San Francisco the night before they arrived here. They expect not just good food, but great food.

Before I came to the Ranch, I thought I would draw heavily from my original training in classical French and Continental cuisines, taught to me by my first mentor, Luis Luzzati, former chef to England's Princess Margaret. Maybe I'd also toss in a little ol' Rocky Mountain High food style (high fat, no doubt) as well. Surely my bag of tricks would see me through.

No way. Gone…all gone as possible techniques the moment I walked in the door here. Also out of the question: those less lofty but still high-fat and calorie-laden California and Southwest themes.

In their place, a healthy interpretation of vegetarian cuisine that is uniquely Rancho La Puerta. Specifics about caloric content and fat limitations became second nature to me. At cooking classes I'd be asked stumpers like, "Does the pigment anthocyanin in eggplant trigger our blood vessels to dilate?" At first, I didn't have a clue. So I read. I studied. I buried my chromed head in enough health and nutrition newsletters from top-line institutions to fill a small library. I asked lots of questions. Soon I could recite the fat grams in any portion and tell you that, yes, anthocyanin is a dilator and is also found in red and purple grapes.

The more I cooked with local ingredients and healthier techniques, the more I was won over by this cooking style. Sure, at first I still craved a grilled veal chop smothered in Bordelaise sauce with chanterelles, paired with pommes Anna, asparagus, and a dollop of Sauce Smitane every now and then (forgive me!), but even those memories were fading.

Soon I was preparing close to 170,000 meals a year. It sounds like a great number, but even meals for only 150 spa-goers each week do add up! When possible everything came from our organic gardens, and I was without the "aid" of any animal product except low-fat or skim milk products and egg whites. I do serve fresh fish and seafood three times a week, so I've come to enjoy the "rules" of this healthy cuisine as well. What are the rules? I seldom use wines or liquors, and never butter, cream, or beef, chicken, duck, pork or veal stocks. In the beginning I worried that I was up against a very high wall. Vegetable stock only? A diet limited to 1,500 mg of salt or sodium per day and fat levels below 18 percent? I know now that the answer is yes! I can do it. And you can do it too, even in your own kitchen.

Over the years I've played with many recipes, always refining and experimenting. My amounts and instructions are not meant to be clinical, and I hope you'll enjoy each dish's simple style: seasonally fresh, low in fat, high in fiber, nutritionally tasty, and easy to prepare. My highest hope is that this book will become tattered and scrawled upon, and each page's top corner bent from use in your kitchen. I hope it feels the sweep of an ostrich feather duster less than most.

Throughout the book I've included my hints on food selection, unusual preparation tips, favorite ingredients, and some plain ol' personal opinion. You hold the secrets of Rancho La Puerta cooking in your hands right now. These are the recipes that guests ask for over and over again to take home.

We've also included some descriptions of what my colleagues, the fitness professionals at the Ranch, also inspire in our guests: how to "take the Ranch home." Their advice on stretching, relaxation, exercise, and the mind/body/spirit connection, is invaluable.

Looking back now on the years here, I wonder why I hadn't caught on to this healthy style well before I entered the spa world of Deborah and Alex. I was raised by my grandparents, and my Colorado cowboy, farmer, casino-proprietor, vegetable-juice–drinking, Prevention magazine-readin', Swiss-German grandpa Henry "Hank" Fehlman was the healthiest person I've ever known.

My earliest memory of Grandpa is of his driving me to school in the farm pickup, snowing to beat all hell, heater running full blast, windows rolled up, and Grandpa doling out the facts of ranch life while reaching into his pocket for some garlic. Every morning he stashed a handful or two of peeled cloves in his pants so he could pop one or two in his mouth at certain times. Summer or winter, I'd see him chomping on those little garlic nips while working his land or riding his horse in the Colorado High Country. He was a real vegetable-eating man in a time and place where eating habits like that branded you as eccentric. After hearing about the benefits of vegetable juicing from no less than health-guru Norman Walker himself, Hank changed the way he lived from being a cigar-smoking, highball-drinking tough old gentleman. As he did with everything in life, Grandpa went at his newfound challenge at full speed.

It took me just twenty years and a big push from Deborah to get me focused on the same fork in the road. Here we are together again Grandpa, at last.

The

Rancho La Puerta

Cookbook

Breakfast

AFTER THEIR EARLY-MORNING HIKES *on Pilgrim's Way or on one of the Ranch's other mountain trails, guests come off a fairly long fast since dinner, and they are hungry! They need to replenish wisely with good-tasting, nutritional fuels, so each day we set out whole-grain toast, muffins, freshly made fruit butters, hot and dry multigrain cereals, and our homemade granola. Also on offer are cut fresh seasonal fruits, yogurt, just-squeezed juices, and herbal teas and coffee. For those needing something even more substantial, we have eggs, either the scrambled whites with fresh herbs or hard-boiled.*

Guests who take the morning garden tour get there by hiking several miles over gentle rolling hills and passing through the many oak groves along a stream. At the Tres Estrellas kitchen they feast on our Garden Eggs served with warm, fresh homemade tortillas, salsas, fresh fruits, and juices.

After breakfast either inside the sunlit casita's main room or outside on the patio, guests head off for a tour of the organic vegetable gardens and orchards with Enrique Ceballos, our resident master gardener and philosopher on nature and love. As everyone leaves for the walk back to the main Ranch grounds, they're full of wonder and respect for what organic gardening can accomplish, as well as energized and ready for the day.

All of our breakfast items can be found on these pages. Take on the day!

Taking the Ranch Home

Siempre mejor—Always better! This has been the Ranch motto since day one, over half a century ago. In the spirit of *siempre mejor,* one of the best-attended seminars at Rancho La Puerta each week is a free-ranging inspirational lecture on "How to Take the Ranch Home."

Hosted by a fitness staff member—and sometimes by Deborah Szekely herself—the talk helps guests take an honest look at what their everyday fitness was at home. Now that they've been at the spa for a week, guests have a great running start on any changes they need to make. How does one keep up the momentum?

Many of the most popular and useful tips from these seminars are scattered throughout this book. Each simple idea is a worthy adjunct to the Ranch's recipes. Returning guests frequently tell staff that, by adopting only one or two of the fitness tips they received, they changed their fitness level and attitude profoundly. *Siempre mejor!*

Rancho La Puerta Granola

Most granolas have far too much fat in them to make them healthy. This one is sweetened with apple juice and a little canola oil is used to hold it together. I can't begin to tell you how popular this granola is at breakfast time and other times. It's so popular that small bags of granola are the most sought-after prize at evening bingo games. Use low oven heat to ensure that the granola doesn't burn. If the edges do burn, discard the charred parts—the rest will be fine!

3 cups old-fashioned rolled oats
1/2 cup chopped almonds
1/2 cup sunflower seeds
1/4 cup whole wheat flour
1/4 cup oat bran
1 tablespoon ground cinnamon
3/4 teaspoon ground ginger
3/4 teaspoon ground cardamom

3/4 cup honey
1/2 cup unsweetened, unfiltered apple juice
2 tablespoons vanilla extract
2 teaspoons canola oil
2 teaspoons grated orange zest
2 tablespoons fresh orange juice (optional)

Per Tablespoon:
25 calories
1 g total fat (34% of calories)
0 g saturated fat
0 mg cholesterol
1 g protein (9% of calories)
4 g carbohydrates (57% of calories)
0 g fiber
0 mg sodium
Makes about 6 cups

1. Preheat the oven to 250°F. Lightly coat a baking sheet with vegetable oil spray.

2. In a large mixing bowl, combine the rolled oats, almonds, seeds, flour, oat bran, cinnamon, ginger, and cardamom.

3. In another bowl, whisk together the honey, apple juice, vanilla and oil until the honey is thoroughly incorporated. Add the orange zest and the orange juice, if desired.

4. Pour the wet ingredients over the dry ingredients and mix well. Spread the granola evenly over the baking sheet and bake for 1 1/2 to 2 hours, checking every 15 minutes. When the granola starts to brown, stir gently with a spatula. Take care that the outside edges do not burn. When golden and dry, scrape onto a plate or a cool baking sheet and set aside to cool. Store in an airtight container until ready to use.

Cinnamon Oatmeal

I add cinnamon and vanilla to the hot cereals I serve at the Ranch, a practice that occasionally has guests wondering what kind of grain I use. It's just one of the secrets to adding a little extra taste. Some of the grains may be unfamiliar to you, but try them. You'll find them a welcome change.

1/2 teaspoon ground cinnamon
1 teaspoon vanilla extract
1 cup old-fashioned rolled oats

1. In a saucepan, combine 2 cups water with the cinnamon and vanilla and bring to a boil over high heat. Reduce the heat to a simmer and stir in the oats.

2. When the mixture starts to simmer, turn off heat, cover, and let stand for 15 minutes, until thick and creamy. Stir once and then serve.

VARIATIONS:

Following are six grains I cook frequently. Add the cinnamon and vanilla for sweeter cereal, or leave them out. Rinse all grains (except oats) before cooking by putting the measured amount in a colander and rinsing it under cold running water. Drain before cooking.

Brown rice: 1/2 cup rice to 1 cup of water. Combine the rice and water in the saucepan and bring to a boil over high heat. Reduce the heat and simmer slowly for about 35 minutes, stirring occasionally, until the water is absorbed. Makes about 1 1/2 cups.

Per Serving (of oatmeal):
80 calories
1 g total fat (14% of calories)
0 g saturated fat
0 mg cholesterol
3 g protein (2% of calories)
14 g carbohydrates (84% of calories)
2 g fiber
6 mg sodium
Makes about 2 cups; 4 servings

Cracked wheat: 1 cup cracked wheat to 2 cups of water. When the grain and water mixture begins to simmer, turn off the heat, cover, and let stand for 25 minutes, until thick and creamy. Stir once and then serve. Makes about 2 cups.

Kasha: 1/2 cup kasha to 3 cups of water. When the water boils, stir in the kasha, reduce the heat, and simmer slowly for about 20 minutes, stirring occasionally, until thick and creamy. Makes about 1 1/2 cups.

Millet: 1 cup millet to 2 cups of water. When the water boils, stir in the millet, reduce the heat, and simmer slowly for about 20 minutes, stirring occasionally, until thick and creamy. Makes about 2 cups.

Quinoa: 1/2 cup quinoa to 1 cup water. Combine the quinoa and water in the saucepan and bring to a boil over high heat. Reduce the heat and simmer slowly for about 15 minutes, stirring occasionally, until thick. Makes about 1 1/2 cups.

7-grain cereal: 1/2 cup cereal to 1 1/2 cups of water. When the water boils, stir in the millet, reduce the heat, and simmer slowly for about 25 minutes, stirring occasionally, until thick and creamy. Makes about 1 1/2 cups.

Persian Pancakes

A favorite we make at the Ranch that can be served for breakfast or brunch—or as an elegant dessert. The recipe can easily be halved.

2 cups whole wheat pastry flour
2 tablespoons wheat germ
1 teaspoon ground cinnamon
1/2 teaspoon ground ginger
1/4 teaspoon ground cardamom
3 large egg whites

4 cups skim milk
1 tablespoon light brown sugar
1 teaspoon vanilla extract
Pancake Fruit and Cheese Filling
  (page 7)
Fruit Butter (page 8)

Per Serving:
99 calories
1 g total fat (6% of calories)
0 g saturated fat
1 mg cholesterol
5 g protein (21% of calories)
18 g carbohydrates (73% of calories)
1 g fiber
36 mg sodium
Makes 12 servings

1. In a large mixing bowl, whisk together the flour, wheat germ, cinnamon, ginger, and cardamom.

2. In another bowl, whisk together the egg whites, milk, brown sugar, and vanilla. Gently mix with the dry ingredients. Do not overmix or the pancakes will be tough. The batter's consistency should be thin enough so that it can be poured. If the batter is too thick, stir in more milk. Cover and refrigerate for at least 20 minutes or overnight.

3. Lightly coat a large sauté pan or griddle with vegetable oil and heat over medium heat. Ladle a generous 1/3 cup of the batter into the pan to make a 6- to 8-inch pancake. Cook for 2 to 3 minutes, until golden on the bottom. Flip and cook until golden on the other side. Transfer to a warmed plate and cover to keep warm while cooking the rest of the batter.

4. Spoon about 1/4 cup of the filling off-center on each pancake and roll into a cylinder. Place on a plate and serve with Fruit Butter (page 8).

Pancake Fruit and Cheese Filling

This creamy filling for pancakes is also delicious spooned over hotcakes and waffles, or stirred into any hot cereal. I vary the fruits with each change of season in the Ranch orchards, with ripe plums, apricots, persimmons, and pears. Sometimes I even sprinkle in a few dried cherries or cranberries.

2 cups low-fat cottage cheese
1 peach, peeled and diced (mango can be substituted)
1 apple, diced
1 cup diced strawberries
1 medium banana, diced
1 tablespoon honey
1/2 teaspoon ground cinnamon
2 to 3 tablespoons fresh lime juice

In a bowl, combine the ingredients and stir until well mixed, taking care not to mash the fruit. Cover and refrigerate until ready to use.

Per 1/3 Cup:

59 calories

1 g total fat (8% of calories)

0 g saturated fat

2 mg cholesterol

5 g protein (33% of calories)

9 g carbohydrates (59% of calories)

0 g fiber

153 mg sodium

Makes about 4 cups

Fruit Butter

We always have one or more of these butters on hand in ice-chilled crocks at the Ranch's breakfast and lunch buffets. This recipe transforms apples into a delicious spread for muffins and breads, but other fresh fruits can be substituted for the apples. If using berries, mangoes, papaya, or pineapple, reduce the simmering time to as little as five minutes.

4 apples unpeeled, and roughly chopped
1 cup unsweetened, unfiltered apple juice
1/2 teaspoon ground cinnamon
1/2 teaspoon vanilla extract

1. Place all the ingredients in a saucepan and simmer for approximately 20 minutes, until the apples are very soft. Drain and reserve the juice.

2. Transfer the apples to a blender or food processor and puree until smooth.

3. Set a sieve over a bowl and press the puree through with a spatula or wooden spoon. Discard the apple pulp. Adjust the consistency of the fruit butter to your liking with reserved juice. Serve at once or transfer to a lidded container and refrigerate for up to 5 days.

Per Tablespoon:
17 calories
0 g total fat (6% of calories)
0 g saturated fat
0 mg cholesterol
0 g protein (1% of calories)
4 g carbohydrates (93% of calories)
0 g fiber
1 mg sodium
Makes 2 cups

Taking the Ranch Home

We know that breakfast is very important. Talk to any active octogenarian and you usually hear something like, "I've always eaten a good breakfast. I can't start the day without a steaming bowl of oatmeal and fruit."

On waking, you may have fasted for as much as twelve hours. You need to lift your blood sugar and prepare for the day, but not with a sweet roll and the chemical high from coffee, the latter which also irritates an empty stomach. Enjoy toast, fruit, cereals, or even a baked potato with yogurt.

And another tip: if you don't feel hungry when you wake up, you've probably been eating long past the time you should stop the night before.

Onion-Potato Pancakes

Use your leftover mashed potatoes for these pancakes or my Mushroom-Potato Burgers (page 190). Sautéing the onion adds a delicious caramelized flavor. Serve with Chunky Applesauce (page 11).

2 russet potatoes, baked and chilled
1 red onion, chopped
1 red bell pepper, stemmed, seeded, and chopped
1/2 cup fresh corn kernels
3 garlic cloves, minced
1/2 teaspoon chopped fresh rosemary
1 teaspoon chopped fresh oregano
2 large egg whites
Salt and freshly ground black pepper

1. Peel the baked potatoes with a paring knife and gently grate them with a cheese grater. Set aside.

2. Spray a pan lightly with vegetable oil spray. Sauté the onion and red pepper over medium-high heat for about 5 minutes, until the onion softens. Add the corn, garlic, and herbs and cook for 2 or 3 minutes longer, until the onion is golden brown.

3. Transfer to a bowl, add the egg whites and potatoes, and mix gently. Season to taste with salt and pepper and form into eight 2-inch patties.

4. Heat a nonstick griddle or a skillet lightly sprayed with vegetable oil over medium heat. Cook the patties for 3 to 4 minutes, turning once, until golden brown. Serve hot with the applesauce.

Per Serving:
110 calories
0 total fat (3% of calories)
0 g saturated fat
0 mg cholesterol
8 g protein (16% of calories)
17 g carbohydrates (81% of calories)
3 g fiber
35 mg sodium

Makes 4 servings

NOTE: *You can substitute raw potatoes for the baked. Submerge the peeled raw potatoes in clean, cool water after grating, then drain and follow the recipe. You will need to sauté the pancakes for 2 or 3 minutes longer.*

Chunky Applesauce

Chopped apples are cooked in a cup of unsweetened, unfiltered apple juice instead of water. The result is so flavorful that I like it as a nonfat spread with toast, and it's the perfect topping for Onion Potato Pancakes (page 10).

3 Granny Smith apples, peeled, cored, and chopped (see Note)
1 cup unsweetened, unfiltered apple juice
1 teaspoon vanilla extract
1 teaspoon ground cinnamon
1 tablespoon light brown sugar
1/4 cup raisins

Put the apples, apple juice, vanilla, cinnamon, brown sugar, and raisins in a small saucepan and simmer very slowly, stirring, for about 15 minutes or until the apples and raisins are soft and most of the liquid has evaporated. Set aside to cool. Serve warm or chilled.

Per Tablespoon:
23 calories
0 g total fat (2% of calories)
0 g saturated fat
0 mg cholesterol
0 g protein (2% of calories)
6 g carbohydrates (96% of calories)
1 g fiber
1 mg sodium
**Makes about
1 1/4 cups**

NOTE: *I like to use Granny Smith apples because they taste wonderful and don't fall apart when cooking, but you can use any firm, tart apple.*

Ranch-Fried Potatoes

Here's a healthful alternative to greasy hash browns or country-fried potatoes at breakfast. I rely on some pretty heady flavors—such as garlic and jalapeño—to make these just as delicious as any potatoes you've had at a diner. Sometimes I also add pinches of fresh thyme and lavender, and I've been known to substitute epazote, *a Mexican herb, for the oregano. Look for it in Mexican and Latin American markets, or grow your own.*

2 russet potatoes, cut into 1-inch cubes

1/2 teaspoon olive oil

1 red onion, chopped

1 red bell pepper, stemmed, seeded, and chopped

1 green bell pepper, stemmed, seeded, and chopped

1/4 teaspoon minced jalapeño pepper

3 garlic cloves, minced

1 tablespoon chopped fresh oregano

1/4 teaspoon ground cumin

Salt and freshly ground black pepper

1. Put the potatoes in a large saucepan and add enough water to cover by about 1 inch. Lightly salt the water. Bring to a boil, reduce the heat, and simmer for 8 to 10 minutes, until fork-tender but not soft. Drain and cool under running cold water. Set aside.

2. In a large skillet, heat the oil over medium-high heat. Sauté the onion, bell peppers, jalapeño, and garlic for 6 or 7 minutes, until the onion and peppers soften. Add the potatoes, oregano, and cumin and season to taste with salt and pepper. Toss for about 2 minutes, until the potatoes are heated through. Adjust the seasonings and serve hot.

Per Serving:

82 calories

1 g total fat (10% of calories)

0 g saturated fat

0 mg cholesterol

2 g protein (10% of calories)

17 g carbohydrates (80% of calories)

3 g fiber

6 mg sodium

Makes 4 servings

NOTE: *The potatoes can be cooked in the simmering water ahead of time, drained, and kept refrigerated for 2 days.*

Garden Eggs with Herbed Tofu

We serve this egg white and vegetable scramble to Ranch guests who have made the morning hike up the valley to see our Tres Estrellas vegetable garden and orchards. They especially enjoy this dish with fresh salsa and hot corn tortillas while sitting on our little garden kitchen's patio. It's low in fat but hearty enough to satisfy even the hungriest hiker.

1/2 teaspoon olive oil

1/2 medium onion, diced

1/2 medium zucchini, diced

1/4 carrot, diced

1/2 cup chopped Swiss chard

1/2 medium tomato, diced

1 jalapeño pepper, diced

2 garlic cloves, minced

1/4 teaspoon chopped fresh oregano

1/4 teaspoon chopped fresh thyme

1/8 teaspoon chopped fresh lavender

2 ounces firm tofu, crumbled

1/2 teaspoon curry powder

Freshly ground black pepper

8 large egg whites

4 corn tortillas, warmed

Roasted Salsa Colorado (page 48)

1. In a large sauté pan, heat the oil over medium heat. Add the onion, zucchini, carrot, and Swiss chard and sauté for about 2 minutes. Add the tomato, jalapeño, garlic, oregano, thyme, and lavender and cook, stirring, for about 2 minutes, until the vegetables begin to soften.

2. Scatter the tofu over the vegetables and sprinkle the curry powder on top.

3. Reduce the heat to low and stir in the egg whites, mixing the vegetables and tofu together so that they bind with the egg whites. Season to taste with pepper. Continue to cook, stirring, for 8 to 10 minutes, until the eggs are cooked. Serve spooned over warmed corn tortillas and topped with salsa.

Per Serving (without salsa):

113 calories

2 g fat (13% of calories)

0 saturated fat

0 mg cholesterol

10 g protein (35% of calories)

15 g carbohydrates (52% of calories)

2 g fiber

192 mg sodium

Makes 4 servings

NOTE: *You can warm the tortillas by wrapping the stack in foil and placing them in a warm (250°F to 300°F) oven for about 10 minutes, or lay each at a time in a hot, dry skillet set over medium heat, and cook, turning once, for about 1 minute per tortilla.*

Breads and Muffins

WHAT IS MORE DELICIOUS AND SATISFYING *than a warm, amber loaf of homemade bread? The breads and muffins we make daily at the Ranch are a main topic of discussion among guests who enjoy the moist but low-fat heartiness of our baking. Whole-grain, without additives, Ranch breads are wonderfully delicious—and they carry on a tradition of baking at the Ranch that dates back to our wood-fired outdoor ovens of the 1940s.*

I find bread baking to be fun, relaxing, and even medicinal in its power to recuperate and nourish me. Besides, I get to enjoy the fruit of my labor one slice at a time. Feeling the wonderful silken texture of the dough joins me with all bakers past and present—the process is that unchanged and so basic and alive. Make bread a few times by hand, setting aside your kneading and bread machines, beaters and blenders, and you'll soon answer any of your own questions about bread baking. It's that natural.

In this chapter you'll find our day-to-day favorites, beginning with the classic Whole Wheat Ranch Bread we've made since day one. Try my quick breads, homemade corn tortillas, and muffins, too.

Whole Wheat Ranch Bread

The act of making bread is relaxing and satisfying, and much less costly than going to the local shrink. The tantalizing scent that fills the house as the bread bakes is its own reward.

1/4 cup honey
2 tablespoons (2 packages) active dry yeast
2 tablespoons canola oil
6 1/2 cups whole wheat flour, plus more as needed

1. In a mixing bowl, combine 3 1/2 cups tepid water, the honey, yeast, and oil. Stir and set aside for 5 or 6 minutes, until mixture bubbles and foams.

2. Begin adding the flour, 1 cup or so at a time, mixing with your hands or a wooden spoon until the dough comes together and forms a manageable ball. Turn out onto a lightly floured surface and knead for 8 to 10 minutes, or until your hands come clean when lifted from the dough and the dough is smooth and elastic (see Note).

3. Divide the dough into 2 equal-size pieces and form into free-form loaves. Put the loaves on an ungreased baking pan. Alternatively, shape dough into loaves and put in two 5 by 8-inch loaf pans. Cover with dish towels and set aside in a warm, draft-free place for 40 to 60 minutes, until doubled in bulk.

4. Preheat the oven to 350°F.

5. Bake the bread on the center rack of the oven for about 40 minutes, until the crusts are golden brown and sound hollow when thumped on the bottom. Cool completely on wire racks before slicing.

Per Slice:
73 calories
1 g total fat (11% of calories)
0 g saturated fat
0 mg cholesterol
3 g protein (14% of calories)
15 g carbohydrates (75% of calories)
2 g fiber
2 mg sodium

Makes 2 loaves, each about 22 slices

NOTE: *To test if the dough is well kneaded, insert a clean thumb into the dough and count to 5. If your thumb comes out clean, the dough is kneaded properly and you do not have to add any more flour.*

Store the bread in a well-sealed plastic bag in the refrigerator. It also freezes well if well wrapped in plastic and foil. I like to slice the bread and wrap individual slices for freezing, which I can remove whenever I need them. Unwrap them and let them thaw at room temperature for a few minutes before toasting or using for sandwiches.

Garden Sweet Breakfast Bread

I make this bread at least twice a week and never tire of the aromas that drift from the kitchen out to the garden. Our guests love it, too, as it's one of the most requested recipes. It's a cross between a cake and a bread— sweet, delicious, and reminiscent of a holiday cake but without those cloying candied fruits. The bread toasts beautifully and freezes just as well.

1 1/2 cups whole wheat flour

2 tablespoons plus 1 1/2 teaspoons oat bran

2 teaspoons ground cinnamon

1/2 teaspoon baking soda

1/2 teaspoon baking powder

Pinch of ground ginger

1/2 cup unsweetened, unfiltered apple juice

2 1/2 tablespoons nonfat plain yogurt

2 tablespoons vanilla extract

2 tablespoons honey

1 1/2 teaspoons canola oil

2 large egg whites

1/2 carrot, grated

1/2 cup dried cranberries

1. Preheat the oven to 350°F. Lightly spray two 3 3/4 by 8-inch loaf pans with vegetable oil spray.

2. In a large bowl, combine the flour, bran, cinnamon, baking soda, baking powder, and ginger and whisk 10 to 12 times to mix.

3. In another large bowl, combine the apple juice, yogurt, vanilla, honey, oil, egg whites, carrot, and cranberries and mix well. Fold the wet ingredients into the dry ingredients, taking care not to overmix. (Overmixing toughens the bread.)

4. Scrape the batter into the pans, filling each about three-quarters full. Bake in the center of the oven for about 45 minutes, or until a toothpick inserted in the center comes out clean. Turn out onto wire racks to cool for at least 15 minutes or until completely cool.

Per Slice:

40 calories

1 g total fat (11% of calories)

0 g saturated fat

0 mg cholesterol

1 g protein (14% of calories)

8 g carbohydrates (75% of calories)

1 g fiber

49 mg sodium

Makes 2 small loaves, about 10 slices each

NOTE: *To store the bread, wrap the cooled loaves in plastic wrap and refrigerate for up to 1 week. Well wrapped in plastic and foil, the loaves can be frozen for up to 3 months. Let them thaw in the refrigerator and reheat in low (250°F to 300°F) oven until warm.*

The Rule of Yeast

Yeast is a living organism that is crucial to baking bread. And, like anything living, it responds to warmth and care. This means that the liquid added to yeast doughs should be warm. The warmth helps activate the yeast so that its cells multiply and produce carbon dioxide gas, which in turn is trapped in the network of gluten strands produced in the flour during kneading and rising. Kneading activates the yeast, too, as does the warm kitchen environment so important when the dough is rising.

I follow what I call Bill's Rule of Finger when I add liquid to bread dough. The water (or other liquid) should be 100 to 105°F—which is the temperature that feels comfortable on your skin when your finger is dipped into the water. If the water feels truly hot, don't use it (or let it cool down); if it feels chilly, don't use it, either. Yeast is dormant at temperatures below 50°F and dies at temperatures exceeding 120°F. This explains why it is important to store yeast at a cool room temperature or, better yet, in the refrigerator or freezer. Make sure it is well protected against moisture.

To test that the yeast is still active, proof it. Many bread recipes suggest this as matter of course. To proof the yeast, sprinkle a teaspoon over a cup of warm water, add a pinch of sugar, and let the mixture sit for a few minutes. It should start to bubble and foam. If the yeast lies on the bottom of the cup without a fizzle, throw it out and buy yourself some new yeast.

Poppy Seed Bread

Although they're tiny, poppy seeds pack a noticeable crunch and nutlike flavor cherished by natural foods cooks and Hungarian kringle makers alike. Resist the temptation to use old poppy seeds that have been sitting in your pantry; fresh ones have much more flavor. Serve thin slices of this bread alone or with some fruit butter.

1/4 cup honey

2 tablespoons (2 packages) active dry yeast

2 tablespoons canola oil

2 tablespoons poppy seeds

6 1/2 cups whole wheat flour, plus more as needed

1. In a large mixing bowl, combine 3 1/2 cups tepid water, the honey, yeast, and oil. Stir and set aside for 5 to 6 minutes, until it bubbles and foams. Add the poppy seeds and stir gently.

2. Begin adding the flour, 1 cup or so at a time, mixing with your hands or a wooden spoon until the dough comes together and forms a manageable ball. Turn out onto a lightly floured surface and knead for 8 to 10 minutes, or until your hands come clean when lifted from the dough and the dough is smooth and elastic (see Note).

3. Divide the dough into 2 equal-size pieces and form into free-form loaves. Put the loaves on an ungreased baking pan. Alternatively, shape the dough into loaves and put in two 5 by 8-inch loaf pans. Cover with dish towels and set aside in a warm, draft-free place for 40 to 60 minutes, until doubled in bulk.

4. Preheat the oven to 350°F.

5. Bake the bread on the center rack of the oven for about 40 minutes, until crusts are golden brown and sound hollow when thumped on the bottom. Cool completely on wire racks before slicing.

Per Slice:

75 calories

1 g total fat (13% of calories)

0 g saturated fat

0 mg cholesterol

3 g protein (14% of calories)

15 g carbohydrates (73% of calories)

2 g fiber

2 mg sodium

Makes 2 loaves, each about 22 slices

NOTE: *To test if the dough is well kneaded, insert a clean thumb into the dough and count to 5. If your thumb comes out clean, the dough is kneaded properly and you do not have to add any more flour.*

Store the bread in a well-sealed plastic bag in the refrigerator. It also freezes well if well wrapped in plastic and foil. I like to slice the bread and wrap individual slices for freezing, which I can remove whenever I need them. Unwrap them and let them thaw at room temperature for a few minutes before toasting or using for sandwiches.

Corn Tortillas

Early every morning I walk along a dirt path for about two miles on my way from my house to the Ranch's kitchen. This walk remains a sensual experience for me, from the stars still shining brightly in the clear black, pre-dawn sky to the smell of baking tortillas that fills the cool air from lo-cal tortillarias, or tortilla factories, where corn tortillas are made from lime-treated corn flour called masa harina and water—nothing more, nothing less. When I make tortillas at home, I generally make them from masa (dough) I purchase from a tortillaria, but because you may not have one of these bakeries in your neck of the woods, I provide the following recipe. Once you make them, you will quickly understand the difference between the store-bought brands and homemade tortillas. When I started making my own tortillas, they were never round, but instead resembled the map of Mexico. The women who work in the kitchen with me still laugh at the memory of my clumsy early attempts. But practice helped me and will help you, too. Don't give up.

1 cup masa harina (see Note)

1. Mound the masa harina on a clean countertop and make a well in the center. Add 3/4 cup hot tap water a tablespoon at a time (see Note), mix-ing by hand until the dough has the consistency of putty but is not sticky. If the dough is sticky, rub a little more flour into it. Cover the dough with plastic wrap or waxed paper and set aside to rest for 15 to 20 minutes. Divide into 8 balls and cover again with plastic wrap or waxed paper.

Per Tortilla:
52 calories
1 g total fat (9% of calories)
0 g saturated fat
0 mg cholesterol
1 g protein (10% of calories)
11 g carbohydrates (81% of calories)
1 g fiber
1 mg sodium
Makes 8 tortillas

2. Cut two 8-inch squares of waxed paper and lay a ball of dough between them. Using a rolling pin, roll the ball into a 6-inch round—or use a tortilla press to make the round. Continue with the remaining dough to make 8 rounds.

3. Heat a dry medium skillet over low heat. Lift a circle, still sandwiched between the waxed paper, and peel off the top piece. (If the paper sticks to the dough, it is too sticky and you will have to massage a little more masa harina into it.) Invert the round into the skillet and peel off the other piece of paper. Cook the tortilla for about 40 seconds on each side, until golden. Transfer to a napkin-lined basket to keep warm or put in a plastic bag and cover the bag with a tea towel. Continue to make remaining tortillas.

NOTE: *Masa harina is sold in Mexican markets and many supermarkets serving Latin populations, as well as in specialty shops.*

Use hot tap water for the recipe. There is no need to use boiling or even extremely hot water.

In Mexico, cooled and dry tortillas are reheated by patting them with damp palms and then heating them in a hot, dry skillet for 5 to 10 seconds or over an open flame. Styrofoam tortilla holders are sold in many supermarkets and keep the tortillas warm.

Orange-Corn Muffins

A tasty low-fat muffin is hard to find, but these fit the bill.

2 navel oranges
1/4 cup honey
2 cups unbleached all-purpose flour
1/2 cup stone-ground cornmeal
1 tablespoon baking powder

1 teaspoon salt
1 cup low-fat buttermilk
4 large egg whites
1/2 cup packed light brown sugar
1/2 cup mashed ripe banana

Per Muffin:
169 calories
1 g total fat (3% of calories)
0 g saturated fat
1 mg cholesterol
5 g protein (11% of calories)
38 g carbohydrates (86% of calories)
1 g fiber
312 mg sodium
Makes 12 muffins

1. Preheat the oven to 400°F. Lightly spray a 12-cup muffin tin with vegetable oil spray.

2. Using a small knife or zester, remove enough of the colored part of the orange for 2 grated tablespoons of zest. Peel the oranges and trim the ends. Slice each orange into 6 sections, removing the white pith and seeds.

3. Spoon a teaspoon of honey into each muffin cup, top with an orange segment, and set aside.

4. In a large bowl, combine the flour, cornmeal, baking powder, and salt and whisk 10 to 12 times to mix.

5. In a medium bowl, combine the buttermilk, egg whites, brown sugar, banana, and orange zest and mix well. Fold the wet ingredients into the dry ingredients, taking care not to overmix. (Overmixing toughens the muffins.)

6. Spoon the batter into the muffin cups, filling each about three-quarters full. Bake for 15 to 20 minutes, or until a toothpick inserted into the center of one muffin comes out clean and the tops are nicely domed. Turn out onto a wire rack and serve warm.

Banana-Bran Muffins

To vary these muffins, add one half cup of blueberries, chopped straw-berries, or cranberries in season.

1 1/4 cups whole wheat flour

3/4 cup wheat bran

1/4 cup old-fashioned rolled oats
  (optional)

1 teaspoon baking soda

1 teaspoon ground cinnamon

1/2 teaspoon ground ginger

1 ripe banana

4 large egg whites

1 cup nonfat plain yogurt or
  buttermilk, or 1 1/2 cups skim milk

1/4 cup plus 1 tablespoon honey or
  brown sugar

2 tablespoons grated orange zest

Per Muffin:

119 calories

1 g total fat (5% of calories)

0 g saturated fat

0 mg cholesterol

5 g protein (17% of calories)

22 g carbohydrates (78% of calories)

1 g fiber

103 mg sodium

Makes 12 muffins

1. Preheat the oven to 400°F. Lightly spray a 12-cup muffin tin with vegetable oil spray.

2. In a large bowl, combine the flour, bran, oats (if using), baking soda, cinnamon, and ginger and whisk 10 to 12 times to mix well.

3. In a blender or food processor, combine the banana, egg whites, yo-gurt, and honey and process until smooth. Add the orange zest and pulse just to mix. Fold the wet ingredients into the dry ingredients, taking care not to overmix. (Overmixing toughens the muffins.) The batter should have a pourable consistency; if not, stir in a little more yogurt.

4. Spoon the batter into the muffin cups, filling each about three-quar-ters full. Bake for 18 to 22 minutes, or until a toothpick inserted into the center of one muffin comes out clean and the tops are nicely domed. Turn out onto a wire rack and cool slightly before serving.

Bran-Raisin Muffins

Beginning the day with the right combination of fresh fruit, cereal, yogurt, and breads gets you off to a good start. These muffins fill the bread requirement—and then some. They are high in fiber, low in calories, and you can vary them by adding half a cup of your favorite chopped fruit.

1 1/4 cups whole wheat flour
3/4 cup wheat bran
1/4 cup oat bran
1 teaspoon baking soda
1 teaspoon ground cinnamon
1/2 teaspoon ground ginger
4 large egg whites

1 ripe banana
1 1/2 cups unsweetened, unfiltered
  apple juice
1/4 cup packed light brown sugar
3 tablespoons raisins
1 tablespoon grated orange zest

Per Muffin:

107 calories

1 g total fat (5% of calories)

0 g saturated fat

0 mg cholesterol

4 g protein (14% of calories)

24 g carbohydrates (81% of calories)

4 g fiber

126 mg sodium

Makes 12 muffins

1. Preheat the oven to 375°F. Lightly spray a 12-cup muffin tin with vegetable oil spray.

2. In a large bowl, combine the flour, bran, baking soda, cinnamon, and ginger and whisk 10 to 12 times to mix well.

3. In a blender or food processor, combine the egg whites, banana, apple juice, and brown sugar and process until smooth. Add the raisins and orange zest, and pulse just to mix. Fold the wet ingredients into the dry ingredients, taking care not to overmix. (Overmixing toughens the muffins.) The batter should have a pourable consistency; if not, stir in a little more juice.

4. Spoon the batter into the muffin cups, filling each about three-quarters full. Bake for 18 to 22 minutes, or until a toothpick inserted into the center of one muffin comes out clean and the tops are nicely domed. Turn out onto a wire rack and cool slightly before serving.

Appetizers, Salsas, Dips, and Sauces

LITTLE MORSELS, BITES, AND TASTES—*enjoyed throughout the day—quell the voracious bent to eat too much at any meal. Appetizers start the anticipation of what will be around the next culinary corner!*

At the Ranch, all guests are encouraged to snack wisely and healthfully between meals on colorful assorted "fingerlings" of fresh cut fruits and garden vegetables with tasty nonfat dips or spreads. But you'll find these recipes are nada—nothing!—like those fat- or salt-laden dips often spread on crackers. Enjoy a baked corn tortilla chip with the sweet but zesty bite of Rainbow Salsa Cruda, or dip a crunchy jicama baton into the light green essence of Cilantro Pesto.

At the Ranch's orientation meetings for first-time guests, I always put out bowls of Pea and Broccoli Guacamole Dip surrounded by an array of brilliant crudités and baskets of oven-roasted chips. The guests can't believe the guacamole is low in fat, and I guarantee you, those bowls get pretty clean pretty fast.

While many salsas and sauces are perfect as appetizers or small bites, they can also be spooned over grilled vegetables and grains or tossed in a salad.

Crostini with Roasted Eggplant Caponata

Plump organic tomatoes from the Ranch garden are abundant, and I al-ways sun-dry plenty of them in the warm, high desert Tecate air. Set out to dry on waist-high screened tables, the tomatoes reach perfect texture and flavor in four to six days. Combine their inherent sweetness with the vinegary saltiness of capers and smoky roasted eggplant, and you can see why caponata is my favorite spread. You can also add a teaspoon of minced garlic, a tablespoon of fresh chopped oregano while processing, and 1/4 cup vinegary green pitted olives.

1/2 loaf whole wheat French bread baguette, cut into 1/4-inch slices
1 1/2 tablespoons extra-virgin olive oil
1/2 pound round (Italian) eggplant
1 ounce dry-packed sun-dried tomatoes
1 cup hot Basic Vegetable Stock (page 75) or water
1 tablespoon capers, drained

1. Preheat the broiler.

2. Place the baguette slices on a baking sheet and brush very lightly with olive oil. Toast 6 inches from the broiler, turning once, until golden. Set aside to cool.

3. Preheat the oven to 375°F.

Per Slice:

17 calories

1 g total fat (50% of calories)

0 g saturated fat

0 mg cholesterol

0 g protein (8% of calories)

2 g carbohydrates (42% of calories)

2 g fiber

11 mg sodium

Makes 24

4. Place the eggplant in a shallow baking pan and puncture the skin with a knife or skewer. Bake uncovered for about 45 minutes, or until the eggplant collapses.

5. In a small bowl, combine the tomatoes and stock, and let the tomatoes soak while the eggplant bakes or for at least 30 minutes. Drain.

6. Cut the eggplant lengthwise into quarters and let cool. Scrape the flesh of the eggplant from the skin and transfer to a food processor. Add the drained tomatoes and the capers and process until smooth. Spread liberally on toasts.

NOTE: *The toasts can be stored for up to 6 days in an airtight container.*

Roasted Eggplant Jumbo

These little gems are one of the most requested dishes at the Ranch. When our garden Japanese eggplants come into season, the kitchen ovens are full of these narrow guys roasting away. The next day, I often make a wonderful low-fat dip with the eggplants, or I coarsely chop them and add to a pasta dish or use them to top a soup or salad.

3 tablespoons balsamic vinegar
1 tablespoon teriyaki sauce
1 tablespoon low-sodium soy sauce
1/2 teaspoon olive oil
4 garlic cloves, minced
Pinch of hot red pepper flakes
1 tablespoon finely chopped fresh
  rosemary

1 tablespoon freshly ground black
  pepper
1 round (Italian) eggplant, sliced into
  4 spears, or 2 Japanese eggplants,
  halved

1. In a medium bowl, combine the vinegar, teriyaki sauce, soy sauce, olive oil, garlic, red pepper flakes, rosemary, and pepper and set aside for about 15 minutes to allow the flavors to blend.

2. Spray a baking sheet or sauté pan with vegetable or olive oil spray. Toss the sliced eggplant in the marinade and immediately lay the eggplant spears on the pan and let stand for 15 to 20 minutes.

3. Preheat the oven to 375°F.

4. Bake eggplant on the center rack of the oven for 18 to 20 minutes or until cooked through and lightly toasted. Serve hot or at room temperature.

Per Serving:

39 calories
1 g total fat (15% of calories)
0 g saturated fat
0 mg cholesterol
1 g protein (11% of calories)
8 g carbohydrates (74% of calories)
3 g fiber
44 mg sodium

Makes 4 servings

NOTE: *Do not let the eggplant sit in the marinade or it will absorb too much flavor and taste overpowering—10 to 15 seconds is just about perfect. The marinade is good with other vegetables and with grains and keeps in the refrigerator, covered, for up to 1 week.*

Mushrooms in Herbed Vinaigrette

Choose the freshest mushrooms possible for this appetizer—the kind that literally leap apart if you were to slice them. But don't pick up that knife! You'll want to pop these in your mouth whole. And to preserve their crisp freshness, these simple but elegant 'shrooms, as I like to call them, should not marinate for more than 15 minutes. More is definitely not better in this case.

1/4 cup red wine vinegar
1/4 cup balsamic vinegar
1 shallot, minced
1 scallion, white and green parts, thinly sliced
2 garlic cloves, minced
2 tablespoons chopped fresh cilantro
1 tablespoon chopped fresh basil
1 teaspoon chopped fresh oregano
Freshly ground black pepper
1/2 pound small white mushrooms, cleaned and trimmed

1. In a medium bowl, combine the vinegars, 1/4 cup water, shallot, scallion, garlic, and herbs and season to taste with pepper. Stir and let stand for about 15 minutes for the flavors to blend.

2. Toss the mushrooms in the vinaigrette for a few seconds, cover, and refrigerate for no longer than 15 minutes. Drain in a colander over a bowl to reserve the vinaigrette.

3. Serve the mushrooms with a tablespoon of the reserved vinaigrette.

Per Serving:
37 calories
1 g total fat (10% of calories)
0 g saturated fat
0 mg cholesterol
2 g protein (21% of calories)
3 g carbohydrates (69% of calories)
2 g fiber
113 mg sodium
Makes 6 servings

Taking the Ranch Home

Snacking, or "grazing," revs up the metabolism at times when you may need it most—mid-morning and mid-afternoon. But be sure to make wise choices and eat in moderation. Stick to fiber from fruits and vegetables. Eat a crunchy low-sodium cracker topped with a slice of ripe tomato and a spicy dollop of roasted eggplant. Avoid fats and sugars.

Three-Cheese Vegetable Quesadillas

Our nontraditional use of feta, mozzarella, and blue cheese will surprise quesadilla lovers. The stronger flavors of these cheeses means we can use a mere two tablespoons of the mixture, along with the savory vegetables, in each folded tortilla. Here at the Ranch, Rigo Ramierez sometimes uses chipotle chiles instead of jalapeños because they pack more of a wallop.

1/4 cup crumbled feta cheese

1/4 cup grated part-skim mozzarella
cheese

1 teaspoon crumbled blue cheese

1/2 teaspoon olive oil

1 jalapeño pepper, seeded and diced

1 garlic clove, minced

1/2 medium tomato, diced

1 scallion, diced

1/2 medium zucchini, cubed

1 teaspoon chopped fresh oregano

2 tablespoons coarsely chopped fresh
cilantro

Six 10-inch flour tortillas

Fresh cilantro sprigs, for garnish

Per Serving:

60 calories

2 g total fat (35% of calories)

1 g saturated fat

2 mg cholesterol

2 g protein (12% calories)

8 g carbohydrates (53% calories)

1 g fiber

82 mg sodium

Makes 18 servings

NOTE: *The cheeses can be mixed ahead of time, covered, and re-frigerated for up to 24 hours.*

1. In a small bowl, mix the cheeses.

2. In a medium sauté pan, heat the oil over medium heat. Add the jalapeño, garlic, tomato, scallion, zucchini, and oregano and cook, stirring, for about 2 minutes, until fragrant. Gently stir in the cilantro and set aside.

3. Lay a tortilla in a medium sauté pan set over medium heat or on a hot grill and spoon 2 tablespoons of the vegetable mixture and 2 tablespoons of the cheese mixture on it. Fold the tortilla in half and toast each side for 1 to 2 minutes, until the cheese starts to melt. Set aside, covered, to keep warm. Repeat with the remaining tortillas and remaining filling. Cut each tortilla into thirds and arrange on a serving plate garnished with cilantro. Serve hot.

Two-Bean Tostadas

All the effort needed to making these goes into the easy task of cooking black and pinto beans, and chopping up a little salsa. Assembly couldn't be simpler, and eating the fragile disks out of hand while balancing a pyramid of lettuce, feta, salsa, and a bit of cilantro is half the fun.

6 Corn Tortillas (page 20)
1 cup Mexican Black and Pinto Beans (page 210)
1 head romaine lettuce, shredded
1 cup Rainbow Salsa Cruda (page 33)
2 tablespoons crumbled feta cheese
6 sprigs fresh cilantro, for garnish

1. Preheat the oven to 375°F. Crisp the tortillas. (See Note on page 163.)

2. In a food processor, puree the beans. Carefully spread a tablespoon of the beans over one side of each tortilla. Top with equal amounts of lettuce and sprinkle a full tablespoon of the salsa over the top. Place each tostada in the middle of a salad plate and garnish with a teaspoon of feta cheese and a sprig of cilantro.

Per Serving:
101 calories
3 g total fat (28% of calories)
1 g saturated fat
2 mg cholesterol
4 g protein (15% of calories)
15 g carbohydrates (57% of calories)
5 g fiber
90 mg sodium
Makes 6 servings

Rainbow Salsa Cruda

This is the salsa we make daily in vast quantities at the Ranch.

3 large tomatoes, diced
1 red or white onion, diced
1 scallion, thinly sliced
1 jalapeño pepper, seeded and minced
1 garlic clove, minced
2 to 4 tablespoons chopped fresh cilantro
2 to 3 tablespoons fresh lime juice (juice of 1 lime)
Salt

In a bowl, combine the tomatoes, onion, scallion, jalapeño, garlic, cilantro, and lime juice and stir gently to mix. Season to taste with salt. Serve at once or cover and refrigerate for up to 4 days.

Per Tablespoon:
29 calories
0 g total fat (9% of calories)
0 g saturated fat
0 mg cholesterol
1 g protein (13% of calories)
6 g carbohydrates (78% of calories)
1 g fiber
76 mg sodium
Makes about 2 1/2 cups

Chinese Dumplings with Chives and Ginger

Whirred in the blender, the filling for these dumplings takes only minutes to prepare—but remember to begin marinating the tofu some hours before it is blended with other ingredients. Store-bought wonton wrappers make assembly easy.

3/4 pound firm tofu
Asian Marinade (page 35)
1 cup diced broccoli florets
1/4 carrot, diced
2 garlic cloves, minced
1/4 medium onion, diced
1/4 teaspoon five-spice powder
1 tablespoon low-sodium soy sauce

2 tablespoons white wine
4 large egg whites
1 teaspoon chopped fresh cilantro
Pinch of chile powder
Salt and freshly ground black pepper
Forty 2 by-2-inch wonton wrappers
1 3/4 cups Chive-Ginger Sauce
 (page 36)

Per Serving (not including Chive-Ginger Sauce):
159 calories
4 g total fat (20% of calories)
1 g saturated fat
3 mg cholesterol
11 g protein (26% calories)
22 g carbohydrates (54% calories)
1 g fiber
276 mg sodium
Makes 10 servings

1. In a glass or ceramic dish, combine the tofu and marinade, cover, and refrigerate for 2 or 3 hours.

2. In a saucepan of boiling water, blanch the broccoli and carrot for about 30 seconds. Drain and set aside.

3. In a food processor, combine the drained tofu, garlic, and onion and process for 10 seconds. Add the five-spice powder, soy sauce, wine, egg whites, cilantro and chile powder and process until smooth. Season to taste with salt and pepper.

4. Fill a stockpot three-quarters full with water and bring to a boil over medium-high heat.

5. Lay the wonton wrappers on a dry surface and spoon about 1/2 teaspoon of the tofu mixture in the center of each wrapper. Rub a little water along the edges of each wrapper. Fold in half, pressing to seal.

6. Gently drop each wonton into the boiling water. When the dumplings rise to the surface, remove them from the pan with a slotted spoon. Arrange 4 dumplings in the center of each plate and spoon about 3 tablespoons of sauce over them. Garnish with broccoli florets and carrots.

Asian Marinade

I use this for marinating eggplant, tofu, or just about any other vegetable. It's good when added to rice during cooking—a few tablespoons are all you need.

1/4 cup rice vinegar
1/4 cup balsamic vinegar
1/4 cup low-sodium soy sauce
1/4 cup Basic Vegetable Stock (page 75) or water
4 garlic cloves, minced
1 tablespoon chopped fresh rosemary
1 teaspoon olive oil
1/4 teaspoon hot red pepper flakes
1/4 teaspoon coarsely ground black pepper

In a small glass or ceramic bowl, combine all the ingredients and mix well. Cover and refrigerate for at least 30 minutes to give the flavors time to meld. Use immediately or cover and refrigerate for up to 2 weeks.

**Per Serving
(2 tablespoons):**

16 calories
1 g total fat (33% of calories)
0 g saturated fat
0 mg cholesterol
1 g protein (19% of calories)
2 g carbohydrates (48% of calories)
0 g fiber
240 mg sodium

Makes about 1 cup

Chive-Ginger Sauce

This delicious sauce tastes good with the Chinese Dumplings with Chives and Ginger (page 34), and is equally good over pasta, vegetables, or rice. It was featured with the dumplings in Gourmet *magazine in 1996.*

1/2 teaspoon Asian sesame oil
2 garlic cloves, minced
1 tablespoon minced fresh ginger
2 tablespoons low-sodium soy sauce
1/2 cup sake
1 cup Asian Vegetable Stock (page 77)
2 tablespoons chopped and peeled baked potato
1/4 cup snipped chives

In a blender or food processor, combine all the ingredients except the chives and process until smooth. Add the chives and process for 2 or 3 seconds longer. Serve at once or refrigerate in a lidded container for up to 3 days.

Per Serving
(2 tablespoons):
34 calories
1 g total fat (29% of calories)
0 g saturated fat
0 mg cholesterol
1 g protein (16% of calories)
3 g carbohydrates (55% of calories)
0 g fiber
205 mg sodium
Makes about 1 2/3 cups

Chile Peanut Sauce

When I serve this with Thai Spring Rolls (page 38), I increase the amount of red pepper flakes by a shake or two and add about half a cup of the liquid used to stir-fry the vegetables. If the sauce is too thin, I blend in a portion of peeled baked potato—a great thickener. Serve this over rice or steamed vegetables.

1/4 cup unsweetened, unfiltered apple juice
3 tablespoons rice vinegar
2 tablespoons chunky peanut butter
1 tablespoon low-sodium soy sauce
2 garlic cloves, chopped
1 teaspoon chopped fresh ginger
1 tablespoon chopped fresh basil
1/2 teaspoon brown sugar
1/4 teaspoon hot red pepper flakes

In a blender or food processor, combine the ingredients and blend until smooth. Adjust the seasonings and serve.

Per 1 1/2 Teaspoons:
20 calories
1 g total fat (62% of calories)
0 g saturated fat
0 mg cholesterol
1 g protein (16% of calories)
1 g carbohydrates (22% of calories)
0 g fiber
14 mg sodium
Makes about 1 cup

Thai Spring Rolls

Baked, not fried—can these be as good as ones that do a backstroke through a lake of hot oil? I do know that these are such a big hit with guests that I serve them almost every week.

3 tablespoons unsweetened, unfiltered apple juice

2 tablespoons rice vinegar

2 tablespoons low-sodium soy sauce

1/2 teaspoon Asian sesame oil

4 garlic cloves, thinly sliced

1 tablespoon minced fresh ginger

2 tablespoons chopped fresh basil

1/2 teaspoon canola oil

1/2 red onion, chopped

1 red bell pepper, stemmed, seeded, and chopped

1 yellow bell pepper, stemmed, seeded, and chopped

1 carrot, sliced on the bias into thin slices

1 celery rib, sliced on the bias into thin slices

1/2 pound shiitake mushrooms, stemmed and sliced

1/2 pound fresh white mushrooms, sliced

1 cup shredded red cabbage

2 cups mung bean sprouts

Six 6 by 6-inch wonton wrappers

1 cup Thai Carrot-Ginger Sauce
  (page 40)

Per Serving:

126 calories

1 g total fat (9% of calories)

0 g saturated fat

1 mg cholesterol

7 g protein (14% calories)

27 g carbohydrates (77% calories)

4 g fiber

198 mg sodium

Makes 6 servings

1. Preheat the oven to 350°F. Spray a baking sheet with vegetable oil spray.

2. In a bowl, combine the apple juice, vinegar, soy sauce, sesame oil, garlic, ginger, and basil and stir to mix.

3. In a wok or frying pan, heat the canola oil over high heat until very hot. Stir-fry the vegetables, one at a time, for 2 or 3 minutes each or until they begin to soften. Add about 1 teaspoon of the soy-sesame oil sauce to each batch. Transfer the vegetables to a colander set over a bowl. When all vegetables are cooked, toss them to mix. Let the vegetables drain and reserve the liquid.

4. Lay the wonton wrappers on a dry surface, with a corner of each one pointing toward you. Spoon about 3/4 cup filling near the bottom of each wrapper and roll up halfway. Fold in the sides and continue rolling. Dampen the top corner with water or reserved liquid and finish folding, pressing gently to seal. Lay the spring rolls seam side down on the baking sheet. Bake for 15 to 18 minutes or until lightly browned. Serve with the sauces.

Thai Carrot-Ginger Sauce

The bright orange of frothy fresh carrot juice makes this a visual delight as well as a refreshing source of vitamin A. I sometimes zip up the sauce a bit by adding a fresh chile when blending.

2 cups fresh carrot juice
1/4 baked russet potato, peeled
1/4 cup rice vinegar
2 tablespoons teriyaki sauce
1 tablespoon low-sodium soy sauce
1 teaspoon minced fresh ginger
2 garlic cloves, minced
1/2 teaspoon Vietnamese-style chile sauce
1/2 teaspoon finely chopped fresh rosemary
1/4 teaspoon brown sugar
1/4 teaspoon Asian sesame oil

In a blender or food processor, combine the ingredients and blend until smooth. Let stand for about 15 minutes to give the flavors time to blend. Serve at once or transfer to a lidded container and refrigerate for up to 3 days.

Per Tablespoon:

11 calories

0 g total fat (10% of calories)

0 g saturated fat

0 mg cholesterol

0 g protein (7% of calories)

2 g carbohydrates (83% of calories)

0 g fiber

50 mg sodium

Makes about 2 1/2 cups

Taking the Ranch Home

We're all born with the same body flexibility, but we lose much of it by mid-child-hood. Then matters worsen: by the time we spend another few decades hunched over desks and folded into cars, flexibility is all but gone, especially the ability to squat on our heels with knees up around our ears—or fold ourselves into a comfortable position while sitting or kneeling on the floor.

To maintain or restore flexibility, begin doing passive, gentle stretches while watching the news, eating breakfast, or reading the paper. Gradual, consistent activity will bring about lasting change and become something you don't want to give up. Be aware of your breathing. Relax deeply and discover the universe within.

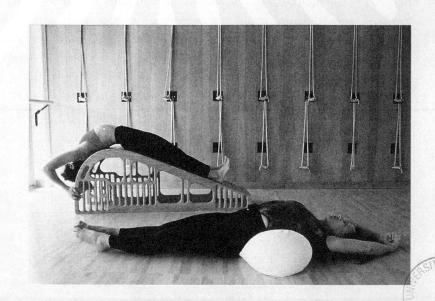

Chipotle en Adobo

A great salsa! The smokiness of the dried chipotle when simmered slowly blends deep into this sauce and renders a taste that is very smooth and oh so tasty. If you cook this salsa at a higher heat, it will boil and break the skins of the chiles. Then watch out! You now have an extra warm, hot sauce that is also very good. Most people like it when simmered slowly. When I do this in my cooking class there is none . . . zero . . . left. I put this sauce over everything. It is especially wonderful with my garden eggs.

4 chipotle peppers, dry

8 tomatoes, chopped

1 onion, julienne

2 cloves fresh garlic, minced

1 tablespoon rice wine vinegar

1 teaspoon brown sugar

1/2 teaspoon sea salt

2 cups water

1 lime, squeezed

Place everything in a saucepan over low heat and simmer for approximately 15 to 20 minutes, until the salsa is thick. Remove the chiles from the salsa and place the remaining ingredients in a blender or food processor with a squeeze from the lime. Stem the chipotles and add as many as you wish depending on your love for chiles. One added renders the salsa slightly warm. Two, warmer. You be the judge! I like it hot, so I add them all! Pulse the blender a couple of seconds until the salsa is slightly chunky. Dip it or spread it on anything. You'll make this a habit. I know you will. Enjoy!

Per Tablespoon:

29 calories

0 g total fat (9% of calories)

0 g saturated fat

0 mg cholesterol

1 g protein (13% of calories)

7 g carbohydrates (78% of calories)

2 g fiber

134 mg sodium

Makes 12 servings

Salsa Not Too Pica

"Not too pica" means not too spicy hot. The cooks in the Ranch kitchen slice a few peeled cucumbers, drizzle some of this on top, and munch away, but I serve it over rice, and vegetables. If you want more spiciness, add a few more chiles de arbol or Thai chiles. But then, of course, it's no longer not too pica.

1/2 teaspoon olive oil
1 chile de arbol or other dried hot chile
2 ancho chiles
4 or 5 plum tomatoes (generous 3/4 pound), quartered
1 medium onion, finely diced
1 jalapeño pepper, stemmed and chopped (do not seed)
1/2 teaspoon ground cumin
2 tablespoons chopped fresh cilantro
Salt and freshly ground black pepper

1. In a large sauté pan, heat the oil over medium heat and sauté the dried chiles for about 1 minute, until lightly browned. Remove from the pan and set aside. Add the tomatoes, onion, jalapeño, and cumin to the pan and sauté for about 5 minutes, until softened. Transfer to a blender or food processor.

2. Remove the stems and seeds from the dried chiles and add to the blender or food processor. Add the cilantro and process for about 10 seconds until blended but still chunky. Season to taste with salt and pepper and serve.

Per 1 1/2 Teaspoons:
9 calories
0 g total fat (17% of calories)
0 g saturated fat
0 mg cholesterol
0 g protein (13% of calories)
2 g carbohydrates (70% of calories)
0 g fiber
2 mg sodium
Makes about 1 1/2 cups

Salsa Verde

A Corn and Feta Soufflé (page 172) wouldn't be the same without a generous dollop of this green salsa. But don't stop there, like other Ranch salsas, you'll find uses for it at every meal.

1 pound tomatillos (about 10 medium), husked and washed
1 medium tomato, quartered
1 medium onion, chopped
2 garlic cloves, chopped
2 toasted chiles de arbol, stemmed (see Note)
1 jalapeño pepper, stemmed and seeded
1 tablespoon chopped fresh oregano
8 sprigs fresh cilantro
Salt

1. In a large saucepan, combine the tomatillos, tomato, onion, garlic, chile de arbol, jalapeño, oregano, and 2 cups water. Bring to a simmer over medium heat and cook for 12 or 13 minutes, until the tomato is soft. Drain, reserving the cooking liquid.

2. Transfer the mixture to a food processor, add the cilantro, and pulse 5 to 8 times, until mixed but still chunky. Add the reserved cooking liquid to adjust the consistency of the salsa. Season to taste with salt and serve.

Per Tablespoon:
19 calories
0 g total fat (16% of calories)
0 g saturated fat
0 mg cholesterol
1 g protein (13% of calories)
4 g carbohydrates (71% of calories)
1 g fiber
49 mg sodium
Makes about 3 cups

NOTE: *To toast dried chiles, skewer them on the end of a long-handled fork and hold over a flame until toasty brown. Alternatively, toast them in a dry sauté pan, tossing until browned. Do not let the chiles burn or they will taste bitter.*

Rosie's 3-Wah Tomatillo Salsa

My wife Rosie makes any number of great salsas. She is from a small fishing village called Zihuatanejo, on the southern Pacific coast in the state of Guererro, which is one of the most gorgeous places on earth. It was there that I met Rosie—and, of course, first tasted her famous salsas. This one uses tomatillos, which are not tomatoes—they're related to gooseberries! I love the tartness they give to a dish, making this sauce delicious with Chiles Rellenos (page 166), burritos, tacos, enchiladas—the list goes on.

1/2 teaspoon olive oil

1/2 medium onion, chopped

2 ancho chiles, stemmed and seeded

1 chile de arbol, stemmed and seeded

10 tomatillos, husked and washed

2 garlic cloves, minced

2 tablespoons chopped fresh cilantro

1/4 teaspoon ground cumin

Salt

1. In a medium saucepan, heat the oil over medium heat and sauté the onion and chiles for 2 or 3 minutes or until the chiles are lightly browned. Lift the chiles from the pan and set aside. Add the tomatillos, 1/2 cup water, and the garlic to the pan and cook for about 15 minutes, stirring, until the tomatillos soften.

2. Transfer the tomatillo mixture to a food processor or blender, add the chiles, cilantro, and cumin, and process for just a few seconds until blended but still chunky. Season to taste with salt and serve. Refrigerate in a lidded container for up to 5 days.

Per 2 1/2 Tablespoons:

11 calories

0 g total fat (22% of calories)

0 g saturated fat

0 mg cholesterol

0 g protein (13% of calories)

2 g carbohydrates (65% of calories)

1 g fiber

15 mg sodium

Makes about 3 to 4 cups

NOTE: *Rosie often adds the kernels from a roasted ear of corn to this salsa. Cook the corn over a grill or open flame until toasty, cut the kernels from the cob, and stir them into the salsa as the very last step.*

Mango Tomatillo Salsa

This salsa accents any grilled foods perfectly—especially grilled vegetables. Make it when mangoes start appearing in the local markets, near winter's end.

1/2 teaspoon olive oil

2 chiles de arbol or other dried hot chiles

1/2 pound tomatillos, husked and washed

1 medium onion, coarsely diced

3 garlic cloves, minced

1 cup Basic Vegetable Stock (page 75) or water

1 large mango (about 8 ounces), peeled and diced

1/4 cup chopped flat-leaf parsley

1 to 2 tablespoons chopped fresh cilantro

1/2 cup fresh orange juice

1/2 cup fresh lime juice

Salt

Per 1/2 Cup:

68 calories

0 g total fat (4% of calories)

0 g saturated fat

0 mg cholesterol

1 g protein (8% of calories)

15 g carbohydrates (88% of calories)

1 g fiber

10 mg sodium

Makes about 3 cups

1. In a small dry sauté pan, sauté the chiles over medium-high heat for about 1 minute, until lightly browned and just beginning to smoke; do not char. Remove from the pan and set aside. When cool, remove the stems and seeds from the chiles and chop coarsely.

2. In a medium saucepan, combine the chiles, tomatillos, onion, garlic, and stock and simmer over low heat for about 15 minutes, until the tomatillos soften. Set aside to cool slightly.

3. Transfer the cooled ingredients to a blender or food processor and process for only a few seconds, until blended but still chunky. Scrape into a medium bowl and add the mango, parsley, cilantro, and juices. Stir gently and season to taste with salt. Serve at once or cover and refrigerate for up to 2 days.

Mango Citrus Salsa

This is a delicious salsa fresca, *or fresh sauce. The deep oranges and yellow hues are beautiful, and the jicama adds a clean, crunchy snap. Try this with fruit salad or grilled vegetables.*

1 large mango (about 8 ounces)
1/2 cup peeled and diced jicama
1 jalapeño pepper, finely chopped
2 tablespoons fresh orange juice
1 grapefruit, segmented
1 orange, segmented
1 teaspoon grated orange zest
1 teaspoon grated lime zest

1. Peel the mango and scrape as much of the flesh from the seed as possible. Put the flesh and any collected juices in a blender or food processor and blend until smooth.

2. Scrape the pureed mango into a large bowl and add the jicama, jalapeño, orange juice, grapefruit sections, orange sections, orange zest, and lime zest and stir gently. Serve at once.

Per 1/2 Cup:

46 calories

0 g total fat (3% of calories)

0 g saturated fat

0 mg cholesterol

1 g protein (6% of calories)

12 g carbohydrates (91% of calories)

2 g fiber

1 mg sodium

Makes about 4 cups

NOTE: *When segmenting the citrus fruits, hold them over a bowl to catch the juices and add the juices to the salsa, too.*

Roasted Salsa Colorado

This spicy salsa has become a favorite of mine. Developed by Christina Cervantez in the Ranch kitchens, it combines the smokiness of a cooked salsa with the crunchiness of a fresh one. Since its first incarnation, we have tamed the fire of this salsa some. I now start with two chiles, while Christina begins with six—and adds more if she feels the salsa needs them.

2 chiles de arbol or other dried hot chiles
5 plum tomatoes
1 medium onion, quartered
2 garlic cloves, minced
1/4 cup chopped fresh cilantro
Salt

1. In a dry medium sauté pan, sauté the chiles over medium-high heat for about 1 minute, until lightly browned and just beginning to smoke; do not char. Remove from the pan and set aside. When cool, remove the stems and seeds from the chiles and coarsely chop them.

2. Add the tomatoes and onion to the pan and cook for about 10 minutes, turning, until the tomatoes and onion are well browned and start to fall apart.

3. Transfer the tomatoes and onion to a blender or food processor, add the chiles, and process just until blended but still chunky. Scrape into a bowl, stir in the garlic and cilantro, and season to taste with salt.

Per 2 1/2 Tablespoons:
10 calories
0 g total fat (10% of calories)
0 g saturated fat
0 mg cholesterol
0 g protein (15% of calories
2 g carbohydrates (75% of calories)
1 g fiber
31 mg sodium
Makes about 1 1/2 cups

NOTE: *If you plan to use this to coat the tortillas for chiles rellenos or enchiladas, process it a little longer to make it easier to roll the tortillas.*

When browning the tomatoes and onion, be sure to turn on the kitchen fan, as the vegetables will smoke. In Mexico, cooks char the vegetables until they are black and the room is filled with smoke. They also add the same number of chiles as tomatoes, preferring their salsas very hot and spicy

Ancho Chile Sauce

Ancho and California chiles add a not-too-spicy flavor to a sauce that becomes irresistible around a bowl of chips, or placed ready to spoon over enchiladas, quesadillas, or chiles rellenos.

5 dried California chiles
4 ancho chiles
1 small jalapeño pepper
2 cups Basic Vegetable Stock (page 75) or water
1 medium onion, diced
10 tomatillos, husked, washed, and quartered
2 medium tomatoes, quartered
3 garlic cloves, chopped
1 teaspoon chopped fresh cilantro
Salt and freshly ground pepper

1. In a dry medium sauté pan, sauté the chiles and jalapeño over medium-high heat for about 1 minute, until lightly browned and just beginning to smoke; do not char. Remove from the pan and set aside. When cool, remove the stems and seeds from the dried chiles and coarsely chop all the chiles.

2. In a large saucepan, combine the stock, onion, tomatillos, tomatoes, garlic, and chiles and bring to a boil over medium-high heat. Reduce the heat and simmer for about 10 minutes, uncovered, until the tomatoes are soft. Drain in a sieve set over a bowl to collect the liquid.

3. Transfer the drained vegetables to a food processor or blender and pulse a few times, until the mixture is blended but still chunky. Scrape into a medium bowl and adjust the consistency with the reserved cooking liquid. Stir in the cilantro and season to taste with salt and pepper. Serve at once or cover and refrigerate for up to 4 days.

Per 2 Tablespoons:
44 calories
1 g total fat (11% of calories)
0 g saturated fat
0 mg cholesterol
2 g protein (14% of calories)
8 g carbohydrates (75% of calories)
1 g fiber
348 mg sodium
Makes about 3/4 cup

Tomato-Basil Sauce

If tomatoes are in season, then so is basil and it's time to make a sauce using both. Spread this on freshly baked bread or focaccia for a hearty appetizer.

1/2 teaspoon olive oil
1/2 medium onion, chopped
4 garlic cloves, chopped
4 medium tomatoes, chopped
1/4 cup chopped fresh basil
Freshly ground black pepper

1. In a large saucepan, heat the oil over medium heat and sauté the onion for about 5 minutes, until golden. Add the garlic and tomatoes, and sauté for about 2 minutes, until the tomatoes begin to soften. Add the basil and simmer for about 1 minute, until the basil wilts.

2. Transfer to a food processor or blender and process for a few seconds until blended but still chunky. Season to taste with pepper and serve.

Per 1/2 Cup:

20 calories

1 g total fat (20% of calories)

0 g saturated fat

1 mg cholesterol

1 g protein (13% of calories)

7 g carbohydrates (67% of calories)

1 g fiber

159 mg sodium

Makes about 2 cups

Sun-Dried Tomato Sauce

Sun-dried tomatoes are full of flavor and impart a zippy freshness, too. Although we sun-dry our own tomatoes and herbs at the Ranch and then store them in large zippered plastic bags, we never pack the tomatoes in oil. We rehydrate them in vinegar or stock. I use this sauce over pasta, rice, and grilled vegetables.

1/2 teaspoon olive oil
1/2 medium onion, chopped
1/2 celery rib, chopped
1/2 carrot, chopped
2 shallots, minced
4 garlic cloves, minced
4 medium tomatoes, chopped
2 ounces dry-packed sun-dried tomatoes
2 tablespoons chopped fresh basil
Freshly ground black pepper

1. In a large saucepan, heat the oil over medium heat and sauté the onion, celery, carrot, and shallots for about 5 minutes, until the onion is golden. Add the garlic, ripe tomatoes, and sun-dried tomatoes and sauté for 2 minutes longer. Add 1 cup of water and the basil, and simmer for about 15 minutes, until the tomatoes soften.

2. Transfer to a food processor or blender and process for a few seconds, just until blended but still chunky. Season to taste with pepper and serve.

Per 1/4 Cup:
36 calories
1 g total fat (13% of calories)
0 g saturated fat
0 mg cholesterol
2 g protein (15% of calories)
8 g carbohydrates (72% of calories)
2 g fiber
155 mg sodium
Makes about 2 1/2 cups

Ranch Pesto

Here is a pesto you can enjoy as is or and you can tailor it to your own taste. Substitute roasted red bell peppers or sun-dried tomatoes for the spinach or add a chile de arbol for a little zip. I toss this pesto with pasta and add stir-fried peppers, zucchini, onions, and mushrooms seasoned with garlic and oregano. A little grated Parmesan never hurts, either.

1/3 cup shelled pumpkin seeds (about 1 ounce)
10 garlic cloves
2 cups chopped fresh basil
6 cups chopped fresh spinach
1 cup chopped fresh flat-leaf parsley
1/2 cup chopped fresh oregano
1/4 cup finely grated Parmesan cheese
1/4 cup olive oil
1/4 cup fresh lime juice

1. In a small sauté pan, toast the pumpkin seeds over medium heat for about 1 minute, until lightly browned. Transfer to a plate to cool.

2. In a food processor, combine the pumpkin seeds and the other ingredients and process until smooth. Scrape into a dish, cover, and refrigerate until ready to use.

Per Tablespoon:
28 calories
2 g total fat (68% of calories)
0 g saturated fat
1 mg cholesterol
1 g protein (10% of calories)
2 g carbohydrates (21% of calories)
1 g fiber
18 mg sodium
Makes about 2 cups

Cilantro-Garlic Sauce

Developed by Aurora Ramirez, a cook in the Ranch kitchen, this sauce features cilantro, lemon juice, and garlic. We serve it with tofu and grilled vegetables.

1 teaspoon olive oil
10 garlic cloves, minced
2 cups white wine
2 cups chopped fresh cilantro
1/4 cup fresh lemon juice
2 tablespoons low-sodium soy sauce
1 teaspoon cornstarch

1. In a medium sauté pan, heat the oil over medium-high heat and cook the garlic for about 1 minute. Add the wine and simmer for 2 or 3 minutes. Add the cilantro, lemon juice, and soy sauce and stir gently to blend.

2. In a small dish, combine the cornstarch with 3 tablespoons water and stir until the cornstarch dissolves. Stir into the simmering sauce to thicken, cooking for about 1 minute. Do not boil. Serve immediately.

Per Tablespoon:
19 calories
0 g total fat (27% of calories)
0 g saturated fat
0 mg cholesterol
0 g protein (12% of calories)
1 g carbohydrates (61% of calories)
0 g fiber
42 mg sodium
Makes about 1 1/2 cups

Vietnamese Spicy Hot Chile Sauce

This may sound like a lot of chiles—and it is—but this sauce keeps for a while and you'll find yourself using it with pastas, salads, soups and lots more (which explains why I recommend making it in such quantity). When I was in Vietnam in the late 1960s, I was intrigued by the rustic roadside soup stands where there were always fresh and dried chiles hanging from the rafters. These were used to make all sorts of sauces that, with sugary vinegars, were used as condiments for the array of delicious soups. This sauce tastes close to those sauces, as I recall. I also make a slightly sweeter version with toasted chiles.

50 chiles de arbol or other dried hot chiles, stemmed
1/4 cup rice vinegar
10 garlic cloves, minced
1 teaspoon sugar
1 teaspoon salt

In a large saucepan, combine the ingredients, add 2 cups water, and cook over medium-low heat for 15 to 20 minutes, until the chiles are soft. Transfer to a food processor and process until smooth. Season with more vinegar and salt, if necessary. Refrigerate in a lidded container for up to 2 weeks.

Per Tablespoon:

26 calories

0 g total fat (4% of calories)

0 g saturated fat

0 mg cholesterol

2 g protein (16% of calories)

6 g carbohydrates (80% of calories)

1 g fiber

48 mg sodium

Makes about 2 cups

NOTE: *You can halve the recipe.*

Shiitake-Tomatillo Sauce

East meets Mexico in this unusual sauce. The delicate smokiness of shiitake mushrooms goes well with the tartness of fresh tomatillos. Papery-husked tomatillos are found in Latin produce markets and make great salsas (Rosie's Z-wah Tomatillo Salsa, page 45). At the Ranch, we spoon this sauce over Roasted Tamale Pie (page 168).

2 pounds tomatillos, husked and washed (see Note)

2 cups Basic Vegetable Stock (page 75)

4 garlic cloves, minced

1/4 teaspoon olive oil

1 medium onion, chopped

1 leek, well washed and sliced (see Note)

2 tablespoons chopped fresh oregano leaves

1/2 pound shiitake mushrooms, stemmed and thinly sliced

2 roasted red bell peppers (pages 58–59)

Salt and freshly ground black pepper

Per Tablespoon:
57 calories
1 g total fat (13% of calories)
0 g saturated fat
0 mg cholesterol
2 g protein (15% of calories)
12g carbohydrates (72% of calories)
2 g fiber
155 mg sodium
Makes about 3 cups

1. In a medium saucepan, combine the tomatillos, stock, and half of the garlic and simmer over medium heat for about 15 minutes, or until the tomatillos soften. Transfer to a sieve set over a bowl and set aside to drain.

2. In a large sauté pan, heat the oil over medium heat and sauté the onion, leek, remaining garlic, and oregano for about 5 minutes, until the onion begins to soften. Add the mushrooms and cook for about 5 minutes longer, until the mushrooms soften. Set aside.

3. In a blender, combine the tomatillos, red peppers, and a little of the drained liquid from the tomatillos and blend until smooth. (Take care if the tomatillos are still hot.) Add this mixture to the mushroom mixture, season to taste with salt and pepper, and bring to a simmer over low heat. When heated through, serve.

NOTE: *You can substitute green tomatoes for the tomatillos, although the flavor will not be the same. When cleaning the leek, rinse it well, slice vertically, and soak in cold water to remove the sand and grit. Drain and slice.*

Selecting and Roasting Chiles

When I explain how much I depend on chiles in my cooking, some folks shudder while others applaud. "How can I eat that spicy food?" the first group asks, while the second group cries, "the hotter the better!" Both groups are ill-informed about chiles, one of the most versatile of vegetables—which perhaps could be considered more of a flavoring agent than vegetable. Chiles range from sweet and mild to fiery. They provide far more than heat in numerous dishes, including the Mexican fare I tend to cook as well as dishes from other culinary traditions. These little gems provide depth of flavor, subtlety, and interest—and, yes, very often intense heat!

The heat is found in the capsicin, a volatile oil in the seeds, and so if you prefer less heat, scrape out all the seeds, regardless of what a recipe instructs. Also keep in mind that heat gathers at the stem end of the chile, while the tip is the least hot.

When working with chiles, take care to keep your hands away from your eyes and mouth. Capsicin can be an irritant, particularly on tender areas of skin. Some cooks like to use latex gloves when working with chiles to protect their hands from burning.

If you eat a chile that is too hot, don't immediately reach for water or beer. The liquid just spreads the inferno. Instead, try a teaspoonful of sugar or a few bites of bread or a tortilla to smother the flame.

While there are hundreds of different kinds of chiles grown in the world, I am primarily concerned with those that apply to Mexican-style food, such as the kind I prepare at Rancho La Puerta, and which are readily available in most markets in the United States.

Ancho: These are dried poblano chiles, which sometimes are called *pasilla* chiles. Deep and reddish brown, anchos are about five inches long and because of how they are dried, are flat and heart-shaped. (*Ancho* means "wide" in Spanish.)

Anchos must be stemmed and seeded and then hydrated in hot water to cover for about 15 minutes. Longer soaking will deplete them of flavor, but a briefer time in the water will leave them leathery. To intensify their flavor further, toast them in a dry skillet before soaking.

Anaheim: A fresh green, very mild chile, anaheims are seven to ten inches long. They are used primarily for rellenos or stuffed chiles. Anaheims should be roasted to remove their skin (instructions follow). Dried Anaheims are known as California chiles.

Cascabel: The seeds inside these nut-brown dried chiles rattle when the chiles are shaken, hence the name, which means "rattle." They are nice and hot, and I add these to salsas for a little zip. Stem and seed these chiles; there is no need to soak them.

Chile de Arbol: These are dried serrano chiles. They are narrow red chiles, only three to five inches long. Chile de arbols are quite hot and even better tasting when toasted in a dry skillet or grilled before they are used. They do not require soaking.

Chile Chipotle: This is my favorite dried chile. It is a peat-smoked dried jalapeño with rich flavor and *mucho* heat. Stem and seed chipotles and then, as with ancho chiles, soak them for about fifteen minutes before using them in soups, sauces, salsas, dips—you name it! Chile chipotle are also sold canned in adobo sauce, a tomato-onion sauce.

Chile Guajillo: This small, dark red dried chile is ubiquitous in Mexican kitchens—and for good reason. It adds a wonderful spicy, nutty flavor to sauces and other dishes, while imparting a brilliant red-orange hue. Stem and seed these chiles; they do not require soaking.

Chile Guero: This fresh pale green-to-white chile is a good substitute for jalapeños. It is quite hot, although not mind-blowing. In Spanish, *guero* means "blond."

Habanero: These fiery fresh chiles currently are a darling among chefs. (They are similar to Scotch bonnets, a hot chile from the Caribbean.) A little bit of these beautiful, vibrantly colored, lantern-shaped chiles goes a long way. Complementing their unprecedented heat is their distinctive citrus flavor, which is extremely pleasing. Habaneros are among my very favorites.

Jalapeño: This is the most widely cultivated chile in the world, and one of the most versatile. The chubby little chiles, which are two to four inches long, range from mildly hot to very hot. They are easily available fresh but are also sold canned, whole, or sliced. Although most jalapeños are bright green, some are red.

Pasilla: See ancho.

Poblano: These are large, heart-shaped deep green chiles that are my choice for rellenos or stuffed chiles. As with anaheims, they must be roasted and peeled. I think their nutty flavor puts them in a league of their own. Some poblanos have a little bite and might need soaking for about ten minutes in warm water mixed with a tablespoon or two of salt to calm them down.

Serrano: These fresh chiles are similar to jalapeños, although they are less fleshy and narrower. Serranos are used throughout Mexico in fresh salsas—and anywhere north of the border where you might find jalapeños. In the Ranch kitchen, we often grill serranos before adding them to salsas.

ROASTING CHILES AND PEPPERS

You can roast chiles and bell peppers in the oven, in the broiler, or over an open flame. In Mexico, where I live, it is a common experience to walk into a neighbor's kitchen only to find it filled with sharp yet fragrant smoke from chiles roasting in open pans or over open flames. Because the smoke might irritate those not accustomed to it, I suggest relying on the oven and broiler methods, only roasting a small number of chiles at a time, turning on the vent fan and, if necessary, opening a window. But don't be dissuaded by this. Roasted chiles are outstanding.

Oven roasting: Put whole, washed chiles or peppers on a baking sheet and bake for approximately fifteen minutes in a preheated 400°F oven, turning once or twice. When the skins become slightly wrinkled and brown, remove the chiles. Set aside and let them cool. Whole chiles steam while they bake, which is why for some preparations and for personal preference, some cooks choose to stem and seed the chiles first and roast them, skin side up, in large pieces.

Once the skins are browned and wrinkled, chiles and peppers can be peeled. While it may be tempting to peel them under running water, resist this because with the water, some flavor washes away. Instead, scrape off the charred skin with the dull side of a paring knife or your fingers, and do not worry if a little bit of blackened skin stays on the flesh.

Broiling: Lay stemmed and seeded peppers skin side up on a broiling tray and broil about five inches from the heat source for a few minutes until the skin begins to brown and wrinkles. Keep an eye on the chiles, because they can burn in a flash and burned chiles are bitter tasting. Let them cool and then peel as instructed for oven-roasted chiles.

Open flame: Skewer the chiles on a long-handled fork and hold them over the flame of a gas burner or grill until the skins are slightly charred. Alternatively, you can set them directly on the burner until the skins brown and wrinkle. As with broiled chiles, flame-charred chiles can burn easily. This is most effective with stemmed and seeded chiles, although whole chiles can be roasted over open flames, too. Make a small slit near the stem ends to allow steam to escape. Let them cool and then peel as instructed for oven-roasted chiles.

Roasted Red Pepper and Corn Sauce

This brilliant red sauce, flecked with yellow corn, fresh oregano, and chopped shallots, comes from Chano Pacheco at the Ranch. Use it over vegetables or in soups as a garnish.

1/4 teaspoon olive oil
2 shallots, chopped
1 garlic clove, minced
1 cup fresh or frozen corn kernels
1/2 cup white wine
1 cup Basic Vegetable Stock (page 75)
2 roasted red bell peppers (pages 58–59)
1 1/2 teaspoons chopped fresh oregano
Salt and freshly ground black pepper

1. In a medium saucepan, heat the oil over medium heat and sauté the shallots and garlic for about 5 minutes, until lightly golden. Add all but 2 tablespoons of the corn, stir in the wine, and simmer for about 10 minutes.

2. Transfer to a blender, add the red peppers and oregano, and blend until smooth. Pour into a small bowl, season to taste with salt and pepper, and stir in the reserved corn. Serve at once.

Per Tablespoon:

14 calories

0 g total fat (9% of calories)

0 g saturated fat

0 mg cholesterol

0 g protein (9% of calories)

2 g carbohydrates (59% of calories)

0 g fiber

2 mg sodium

Makes about 1 1/2 cups

Moroccan Lemons

When Zanne Stewart, food editor of *Gourmet* magazine, told me about this recipe, I quickly found it to be useful in low-fat cooking. The lemons can be prepared in about 10 minutes, but then you need to exercise patience for a week while they cure. The lemons are very salty and a little goes a long way, but they are a great addition to salsas, salads, and other dishes that need a flavor jump. Zanne explained that when cookbook author Paula Wolfert makes these lemons, she stores them in olive oil—but I find I use them so rapidly, I don't need the added fat to preserve the buttery flavor of the lemons.

6 lemons
1/4 cup kosher salt
1/2 cup fresh lemon juice

1. Cut each lemon into 8 thin wedges and lay a single layer of slices on the bottom of a wide-mouthed Mason jar. Sprinkle with salt and layer with more lemon slices and salt. Continue layering and salting until all the lemons are used. Pour the lemon juice over the lemons and seal with the jar's lid.

2. Refrigerate for at least 7 days, turning the jar from side to side several times to mix the juice and lemons. Can be stored in the refrigerator for up to several weeks.

Per Lemon Wedge:

7 calories

1 g total fat (5% of calories)

0 g saturated fat

0 mg cholesterol

0 g protein (9% of calories)

2 g carbohydrates (85% of calories)

0 g fiber

586 mg sodium

Makes about 1 quart

Mongolian Stewed Garlic

I am hooked on these little culinary jewels and once you try them, you will be, too. I got the recipe from my pal, Zanne Stewart from Gourmet magazine, who makes them with Chinese golden rock sugar. I have trouble finding this sugar in Tecate, Mexico, but if you can buy it in an Asian market or specialty shop, substitute it for the brown sugar. I serve these with chips or as a garnish with salads and soups. They keep for a while, but if you prefer, halve the recipe.

64 very large, whole garlic cloves (not elephant garlic), carefully peeled
1 1/2 cups Basic Vegetable Stock (page 75)
1/4 cup low-sodium soy sauce
3 tablespoons rice vinegar
3 tablespoons brown sugar or golden rock sugar

In a medium saucepan, combine the ingredients and bring to a slow simmer over low heat for about 2 hours, stirring occasionally. Do not boil. When the garlic is thick and glazed, remove from the heat and set aside to cool. Serve or store in a lidded jar in the refrigerator.

Per Clove:

7 calories

0 g total fat (3% of calories)

0 g saturated fat

0 mg cholesterol

0 g protein (13% of calories)

2 g carbohydrates (84% of calories)

0 g fiber

31 mg sodium

Makes about 1 quart

Marinated Red Onions

Deborah Szekely, our founder, includes these onions on what she calls the "blitz plate"—a scoop of cottage cheese surrounded by an array of lettuces and blanched, cooled vegetables, which we offer every day for lunch. I love the onions on sandwiches and other cold salads, too. And they take only minutes to make!

1 red onion, thinly sliced
2 tablespoons fresh lime juice

In a small bowl, combine the onion and lime juice, and toss gently. Marinate for 2 or 3 minutes, then serve.

Per 2 Tablespoons:

17 calories
0 g total fat (3% of calories)
0 g saturated fat
0 mg cholesterol
1 g protein (10% of calories
4 g carbohydrates (87% of calories)
1 g fiber
1 mg sodium
Makes 2 servings

Preparing Dried Beans and Legumes

Beans are essential for a good, healthful diet. They are very low in fat and chock full of carbohydrates, protein, fiber, minerals, and vitamins. They are inexpensive, easy to find, and have long shelf lives. Sound like the perfect food? They come close, but nonetheless many folks avoid them, thinking they are difficult to cook because they need to be soaked before they can be cooked.

Beans need soaking to soften them and facilitate cooking. Although the recipes in this book describe the long-soak method, you can also use what is called the quick-soak method. In fact, I prefer it but did not include it as the primary method simply because it requires a little more attention in the kitchen. (When beans are long soaked, they can be left on the kitchen counter, covered with water, overnight or during the day while you are at work.)

To quick soak beans, use two quarts of water for every pound of dried beans. Combine the water and beans in a large pot, cover, and bring the water to a simmer. Let the beans cook at a rapid simmer (not a boil) for five minutes. Turn off the heat and let the beans sit, covered tightly, until cool. When completely cool, drain in a colander and proceed with the recipe. (You can also refrigerate the cooled, undrained beans for eight to twelve hours before preparing the recipe.)

Only beans need soaking. Legumes, which include lentils, split peas, and black-eyed peas, do not. After the beans are soaked, cook them as instructed in the recipe, keeping a few cooking tips in mind, which apply to both beans and legumes.

I never cook beans or legumes in plain water alone. I always use stock or water flavored by onions, garlic, or other vegetables and seasonings. The beans will absorb the flavors. Be sure that during cooking the beans and legumes are *always* covered by at least an inch of water or stock; you may have to add liquid during cooking. This prevents drying and undercooking.

Follow the time guides in the recipes to decide when the beans are cooked, but remember that the cooking time depends also on the age of the beans or legumes—older specimens are drier and will require somewhat longer cooking. As a test, when I think the beans or legumes are ready, I lift a few out of the cooking pot with a slotted spoon and then give them a pinch between my thumb and forefinger. If they are soft and creamy, they are ready for eating.

It's important to cook beans until completely cooked through because not only will they taste better and meld with other ingredients more deliciously, but they are easier to digest. It is generally believed that by incorporating beans more regularly into your diet, digestion becomes easier. Eating them slowly, too, is supposed to aid in good digestion. And finally, I cannot address the issue of digestion without mentioning Beano, a product we serve at the Ranch that can be sprinkled lightly over the cooked food. Beano contains an enzyme that aids in breaking down the oligosaccarides sugars in the beans (the culprits when it comes to digestion). These sugars are essential to beans because without them, the beans could not sprout and propagate. I also find a good walk wearing loose-fitting clothing and comfortable shoes helps digestion.

Cooking times and liquid amounts needed for dried beans and legumes:

Black beans: 1 1/2 hours; 3 cups liquid for every 1 cup beans
Black-eyed peas: 35 minutes; 3 cups liquid for every 1 cup peas
Fava beans: 1 hour; 3 cups liquid for every 1 cup beans
Garbanzo beans: 2 hours; 4 cups liquid for every 1 cup beans
Kidney beans: 1 1/2 hours; 3 cups liquid for every 1 cup beans
Lentils: 30 minutes; 3 cups liquid for every 1 cup lentils
Lima beans: 1 hour; 3 cups liquid for every 1 cup beans
Navy beans: 50 minutes; 3 cups liquid for every 1 cup beans
Pinto beans: 1 hour; 3 cups liquid for every 1 cup beans
Red beans: 1 hour; 3 cups liquid for every 1 cup beans
Split peas: 35 minutes; 2 cups liquid for every 1 cup peas
Soy beans: 2 hours; 4 cups liquid for every 1 cup beans

Hummus sin Tahini

Sin *means "without" in Spanish, and we go without too much fat in this well-known Middle Eastern dressing and dip by losing the tahini—the high-fat sesame seed paste. We still get high fives for this salsa every time it's served.*

1 cup garbanzo beans (chickpeas), sorted and rinsed
1 tablespoon curry powder
1 teaspoon sea salt
1 tablespoon sesame oil
1 roasted red bell pepper (pages 58–59)
2 garlic cloves, minced
1 teaspoon tandoori seasoning (see Note)
Toasted sesame seeds, for garnish

1. Put the beans in a large bowl and add about 10 cups of water. Soak for at least 8 hours or overnight, changing the water a few times, if possible. Drain and transfer to a stockpot.

2. Add 6 cups water, the curry powder, and salt. Bring to a boil over high heat. Reduce the heat and simmer, covered, for about 1 hour or until the beans are soft, with the texture of a baked potato. Be sure the beans are completely covered with water during cooking. (A good test for doneness is to pinch a bean between your thumb and forefinger to test the consistency.) Drain the beans and reserve at least 1 cup of the cooking liquid.

3. Transfer the beans to a food processor and add the oil, red pepper, garlic, and tandoori seasoning. Process until smooth, adding the reserved cooking liquid to adjust the consistency. Serve immediately, sprinkled with sesame seeds, or cover and refrigerate for up to 2 days. Sprinkle with the sesame seeds just before serving.

Per Tablespoon:
30 calories
1 g total fat (26% of calories)
0 g saturated fat
0 mg cholesterol
1 g protein (17% of calories)
4 g carbohydrates (57% of calories)
1 g fiber
66 mg sodium
Makes 2 1/2 cups

NOTE: *Tandoori seasoning is an Indian spice mix available in many supermarkets, specialty stores, and East Asian markets.*

Pea and Broccoli Guacamole Dip

We all love that delicious Mexican classic, guacamole, but it's sooo high in fat and calories that many cooks avoid it and avocados in general. Thanks to a healthy "stretch" in volume and taste given by the peas and broccoli, you can serve this low-fat guacamole with a clear conscience. It has about half the fat content and only a quarter of the calories of traditional guacamole.

3/4 cup broccoli florets
1 cup fresh or frozen peas
1 medium avocado (about 8 ounces), peeled and seeded
1 medium tomato, diced
1/2 red onion, finely diced
1 scallion, trimmed and thinly sliced
1 jalapeño pepper, seeded and minced
2 garlic cloves, minced
1/4 cup chopped fresh cilantro
4 to 6 tablespoons fresh lime juice
Salt

1. In a small saucepan, cook the broccoli in gently boiling water for about 10 minutes, until soft. Add the peas and simmer for about 3 minutes longer. Drain and cool.

2. Transfer the broccoli and peas to a food processor, add the avocado, and process until smooth. Scrape the mixture into a bowl, add the tomato, onion, scallion, jalapeño, garlic, and cilantro and season with lime juice and salt. Mix well and serve or cover and refrigerate for up to 2 hours.

Per Tablespoon:
14 calories
1 g total fat (45% of calories)
0 g saturated fat
0 mg cholesterol
0 g protein (12% of calories)
1 g carbohydrates (43% of calories)
0 g fiber
12 mg sodium
Makes about 2 1/2 cups

Curried Mango-Peanut Yogurt Dip

I based this recipe on one my friend Susan Farmer serves with snow peas from her garden. Mine is lower in fat, but it also tastes great and goes well with snow peas and other vegetables, as well as with pasta.

2 tablespoons chunky peanut butter
2 tablespoons apricot jam
2 tablespoons curry powder
1 cup nonfat plain yogurt
1 large mango (about 8 ounces), peeled and diced
1 red bell pepper, stemmed, seeded, and diced
1 scallion, thinly sliced
1 teaspoon chopped fresh cilantro

In a medium bowl, combine the peanut butter and jam and mix well. Sprinkle with curry powder and then add the yogurt, folding it thoroughly into the mixture. Add the mango, bell pepper, scallion, and cilantro and stir until blended. Serve at once or cover and refrigerate until ready to serve.

Per Tablespoon:

26 calories

1 g total fat (26% of calories)

0 g saturated fat

0 mg cholesterol

1 g protein (15% of calories)

4 g carbohydrates (59% of calories)

0 g fiber

15 mg sodium

Makes about 1 1/2 cups

Alex's Tahini Mustard

I received the recipe for this tasty condiment from Alex Szekely, my boss. It's good on sandwiches, vegetables, rice, and pasta.

5 tablespoons sesame seeds
1/4 cup Dijon mustard
4 garlic cloves
1 tablespoon fresh lime juice
Pinch of cayenne pepper (optional)
Low-sodium soy sauce

In a blender or food processor, combine the sesame seeds, mustard, 1/4 cup water, the garlic, lime juice, and cayenne, if desired, and process until smooth. Season to taste with soy sauce, mix again, and serve or transfer to a lidded container and refrigerate for up to 3 weeks.

Per Serving (1 1/2 tablespoons):
48 calories
4 g total fat (69% of calories)
1 g saturated fat
0 mg cholesterol
2 g protein (18% of calories)
2 g carbohydrates (14% of calories)
0 g fiber
191 mg sodium
Makes about 3/4 cup

Tofu Mayonnaise Spread

This is a terrific low-fat spread or dip that can be varied endlessly by changing an ingredient or two. Give this a shot and dip with vegetables or baked tortilla chips to your heart's content because there is no cholesterol—nada! Always use the freshest tofu possible and buy your tofu from a reliable source.

1/2 cup silken tofu
2 tablespoons fresh lemon juice
1 teaspoon olive oil
1/2 teaspoon minced garlic
Pinch of cayenne pepper
Salt and freshly ground black pepper

In a blender or food processor, combine the tofu, lemon juice, oil, garlic, and cayenne and process until smooth. Season to taste with salt and pepper. Transfer to a lidded container and refrigerate until ready to use or for up to 6 days.

VARIATIONS

Add the ingredients for these variations to the blender or food processor with the tofu and other ingredients. Proceed with the recipe.

Green Goddess Pepper Spread: Add 1/4 cup chopped scallions, 1/4 cup chopped fresh spinach leaves, and 1 tablespoon chopped fresh oregano. Increase the amount of pepper to 1 teaspoon.

Aïoli: Increase the amount of garlic to 2 minced cloves.

Per 2 Tablespoons:

31 calories

2 g total fat (61% of calories)

0 g saturated fat

0 mg cholesterol

2 g protein (24% of calories)

1 g carbohydrates (15% of calories)

0 g fiber

2 mg sodium

Makes about 1/2 cup

Mexican Spread: Add 1/4 cup chopped fresh cilantro and 1/2 teaspoon minced serrano chile.

Sun-dried Tomato Spread: Add 1/2 cup chopped hydrated tomatoes and 1 tablespoon chopped fresh basil.

Herb Spread: Add 1 tablespoon chopped fresh basil, 1 tablespoon chopped fresh oregano, and 1 tablespoon chopped fresh flat-leaf parsley.

Chinese Spread: Substitute Asian sesame oil for the olive oil and add 1 tablespoon tamari soy sauce and 1 teaspoon chopped fresh ginger.

Caper-Mustard Spread: Add 2 tablespoons drained capers and 1 teaspoon coarse-grain mustard.

Soups

I'LL WAGER THAT IF YOU ASK *a hundred chefs around the world what their favorite meal might be, a majority will tell you it's soup! I often make a meal out of the Mexican Vegetable Soup in this chapter, sometimes jumping up the flavor a bit with more chiles.*

Soups, when prepared correctly, are pure and simple but with an underlying complexity of enticing flavors and textures. Ranch "campers" unanimously vote our soups a big hit. We serve two different soups every day, one at lunch and the other before dinner. The bowls routinely return empty. We craft each soup from freshly made vegetable stock, fresh garden vegetables, lots of herbs and garlic … and that's just to start. Depending on the recipe, we may marry this base with a variety of cooked legumes or grains.

Many cooks feel that a soup simply can't be rich and hearty without a beef or chicken stock, but they haven't been to the Ranch. We use zero animal anything, and our soups are delicious.

Mushroom Stock

1 medium all-purpose potato, chopped

1 carrot, chopped

1 medium onion, chopped

1 celery rib, chopped

1 medium tomato, chopped

8 white mushrooms, coarsely chopped

1 head of garlic, skin on, halved

3 sprigs fresh flat-leaf parsley

1 tablespoon chopped fresh herbs, such as oregano, thyme, or rosemary

4 whole peppercorns

2 bay leaves

1. In a stockpot, combine all the ingredients, add 2 quarts of water, and bring to a boil over high heat. Reduce the heat and simmer very slowly for about 2 hours.

2. Strain through a colander lined with cheesecloth into a clean bowl or pan, pressing against the vegetables with the back of a spoon. Discard the vegetables. Cool slightly, cover, and refrigerate for up to 4 days. Or freeze for up to 3 months.

Per Serving (1 cup):

76 calories

0 g total fat (4% of calories)

0 g saturated fat

0 mg cholesterol

2 g protein (11% of calories)

16 g carbohydrates (84% of calories)

1 g fiber

22 mg sodium

Makes about 1 1/2 quarts

NOTE: *Freeze stock in ice cube trays and remove one or two cubes at a time as needed.*

Basic Vegetable Stock

Here's proof that a flavorful stock doesn't have to start with butter and ten pounds of vegetables. I've substituted leeks for the usual one or two yellow onions found in more classic stocks, and boosted the flavor with a generous use of garlic, basil, and oregano.

1 leek, trimmed and chopped	6 garlic cloves chopped
1 carrot, chopped	4 sprigs fresh basil
1 celery rib, chopped	2 sprigs fresh flat-leaf parsley
1 medium zucchini, chopped	2 sprigs fresh oregano
1 medium tomato, chopped	2 bay leaves
1/2 red onion, chopped	6 peppercorns

1. In a stockpot, combine all the ingredients, add 8 quarts water, and bring to a boil over high heat. Reduce the heat and simmer very slowly for about 2 hours.

2. Strain through a colander-lined with cheesecloth into a clean bowl or pan, pressing against the vegetables with the back of a spoon. Discard the vegetables. Cool slightly, cover, and refrigerate for up to 4 days. Or freeze for up to 3 months.

Per Serving (1 cup):

19 calories

0 g total fat (8% of calories)

0 g saturated fat

0 mg cholesterol

1 g protein (14% of calories)

4 g carbohydrates (18% of calories)

1 g fiber

20 mg sodium

Makes 5 quarts

NOTE: *While you can use vegetables other than the tomato, zucchini, and leek suggested here, don't use the cruciferous vegetables (broccoli, cauliflower, broccoli rabe, cabbage, Brussels sprouts); their flavor will overwhelm the stock. Beets will turn the stock red and carrot greens will make it bitter. Otherwise, let your own taste be your guide, adding vegetables such as beans, peas, winter squash, and potatoes.*

Taking the Ranch Home

Incidental fitness—a favorite theme at the Ranch—means working exercise into everyday life. It even happens during guests' "everyday" schedule at Rancho La Puerta as they walk from activity to activity. Deborah and The Professor situated accommodations far from the main gyms and dining room, not only for privacy but also for incidental exercise. Walking at the Ranch adds a mile or two to any daily workout. Yet a pleasant mile it is, keeping pace with the birds that fly from purplish roost to roost in the lavender and Mexican sage bushes.

At home, take the stairs each day instead of an elevator. Walk everywhere you can. Recent research reported by exercise expert and author Dr. Kenneth Cooper confirms that between a control group who went to the gym to workout and those who stayed home and applied their own routines, the homebodies achieved as much as the "temple laborers." If you enjoy gyms, great—use them. But there is no fitness meritocracy open only to gym users.

Asian Vegetable Stock

I use this aromatic stock when preparing Asian-style dishes such as the Miso Soup with Ginger and Garlic (page 80).

4 scallions, chopped

4 celery ribs, chopped

2 leeks, trimmed and chopped

1 carrot, chopped

4 tablespoons coarsely chopped fresh ginger

1 bunch fresh flat-leaf parsley

4 sprigs fresh cilantro

1 sprig fresh oregano

2 star anise

8 peppercorns

1. In a stockpot, combine all the ingredients, add 8 quarts water, and bring to a boil over high heat. Reduce the heat and simmer very slowly for about 2 hours.

2. Strain through a colander lined with cheesecloth into a clean bowl or pan, pressing against the vegetables with the back of spoon. Discard the vegetables. Cool slightly, cover, and refrigerate for up to 4 days. Or freeze for up to 3 months.

Per Serving (1 cup):

21 calories

0 g total fat (8% of calories)

0 g saturated fat

0 mg cholesterol

1 g protein (15% of calories)

5 g carbohydrates (77% of calories)

2 g fiber

20 mg sodium

Makes about 5 quarts

Mexican Vegetable Soup

I cut the vegetables larger than usual in this soup because the result adds some rustic fun and character. We used to make this only for the kitchen staff, but every now and then a guest would wander in and join us with such gusto that I began serving it to everyone. Stirring in a spoonful of Broccoli Potatoes (page 195) just before serving seems to add the right finish.

Per Serving:
42 calories
0 g total fat (6% of calories)
0 g saturated fat
0 mg cholesterol
2 g protein (14% of calories)
10 g carbohydrates (80% of calories)
2 g fiber
66 mg sodium
Makes 6 servings

1 medium onion, cut into 1/4-inch-thick slices
1 celery rib, coarsely chopped
1 carrot, coarsely chopped
1 small red potato, coarsely chopped
1 medium tomato, coarsely chopped
2 garlic cloves, sliced
1 jalapeño pepper, quartered
1 medium zucchini, coarsely chopped
1/2 cup corn kernels
6 cups Basic Vegetable Stock (page 75) or water
1 tablespoon chopped fresh cilantro
Salt and freshly ground black pepper
1 lime, halved

1. In a large saucepan or stockpot, combine the onion, celery, carrot, potato, tomato, garlic, jalapeño, zucchini, corn, and stock and bring to a boil over high heat. Reduce the heat and simmer for 15 to 20 minutes.

2. Add the cilantro and season to taste with salt and pepper and a squeeze of lime juice. Ladle into bowls and stir a tablespoon of potatoes into each serving, if desired.

Tortilla Soup

Once again the secret to cutting fat in Mexican-inspired dishes is to bake ingredients that are usually fried in vegetable oil or (more traditionally) lard. Yet I don't think this soup's garnish of tortilla strips loses a bit of flavor! Another huge fat savings comes in my use of vegetable stock rather than a rich chicken stock. The jalapeño gives the soup a little zing—not too much—and I sometimes like to float a spoonful of Ranch Pesto (page 52) on top. And a last-second squeeze of lime is essential.

Per Serving:

66 calories

1 g total fat (12% of calories)

0 g saturated fat

0 mg cholesterol

2 g protein (12% of calories)

14 g carbohydrates (76% of calories)

3 g fiber

125 mg sodium

Makes 6 servings

2 corn tortillas, cut into thin strips

1/2 teaspoon olive oil

1 medium onion, cut into 1/4-inch-thick slices

1/2 celery rib, chopped

1/2 carrot, chopped

1/4 medium all-purpose potato, chopped

2 garlic cloves, sliced

1 jalapeño pepper, chopped

1/2 medium zucchini, chopped

1/2 cup corn kernels

6 cups Basic Vegetable Stock (page 75) or water, or more if needed

1 medium tomato, chopped

1 tablespoon chopped fresh cilantro

Salt and freshly ground black pepper

1 lime, halved

1. Preheat the oven to 350°F.

2. Lay the tortilla strips on a baking sheet and spray with a little vegetable oil spray. Bake for about 5 minutes, until toasty brown. Do not let burn.

3. In a large saucepan or stockpot, heat the oil over medium heat and sauté the onion, celery, and carrot for about 5 minutes, until the onion is golden. Add the potato, garlic, jalapeño, zucchini, corn kernels, and stock and bring to a boil over high heat. Reduce the heat and simmer for about 15 minutes, until the potatoes are tender. Add more stock or water, if necessary, for the right consistency.

4. Remove from the heat and add the tomato and cilantro and season to taste with salt and pepper. Ladle the soup into bowls, then top each with tortilla strips and a squeeze of lime juice.

Miso Soup with Ginger and Garlic

The only downside of miso is its high sodium content—it can just be too much for some people's diets and/or palates. But the taste, especially with the simple addition of carrots and shiitake mushrooms, is extraordinary. This is an easy introduction to miso, a fermented soy product rich in protein, calcium, potassium, and vitamin A.

1/4 cup miso
2 cups Asian Vegetable Stock (page 77)
1 teaspoon minced fresh ginger
1 teaspoon minced garlic
1/2 teaspoon rice vinegar
1/2 teaspoon low sodium soy sauce
1 ounce firm tofu, cubed
1 scallion, thinly sliced
12 enoki mushrooms, for garnish
4 sprigs fresh cilantro, for garnish

1. Dissolve the miso by stirring it into the stock and transfer the mixture to a blender. Add the ginger, garlic, vinegar and soy sauce and blend for about 10 seconds.

2. Transfer to a large saucepan and bring to a simmer over medium-low heat.

3. Divide the tofu and scallion among 4 bowls and ladle the simmering broth over the tofu and scallion. Top with enoki mushrooms and a sprig of cilantro.

Per Serving:
66 calories
2 g total fat (24% of calories)
0 g saturated fat
0 mg cholesterol
4 g protein (24% of calories)
9 g carbohydrates (52% of calories)
2 g fiber
675 mg sodium
Makes 4 servings

Taking the Ranch Home

Shock yourself into passivity! It's a play on words we take seriously at the Ranch. We see guests stop and stare at the mountain, their thoughts of anything else suddenly banished as they think back to a morning hike—the way sunlight burnished the edge of a boulder, a recollection of fragrant sage as they brushed by. Synchronize your life with but a few natural cycles (When was the last time you looked for Orion in a moonless sky? Or been to the beach at its lowest tide of the year?) and you will soon feel a certain confident stillness and well-being take hold.

Vegetable Barley Soup

In the winter I serve this soup a bit thicker, while in the summer I add a little more stock. Either way, the nutty taste of barley combined with tomatoes is special. Barley will absorb more water than most grains, so you may need additional liquid—stock or water. Use unrefined barley because it is a good source of fiber; you'll find it in health food stores. The pearl barley you see in most markets has had its wholesome bran removed.

2 1/2 pounds tomatoes, coarsely chopped (7 or 8 medium tomatoes) plus 1
   medium tomato, diced

6 cups Basic Vegetable Stock (page 75) or water, or more if needed

1/2 cup barley, rinsed

1/2 teaspoon olive oil

1 medium onion, diced

1 carrot, diced

1 celery rib, diced

4 red potatoes, diced

1 round (Italian) eggplant, ends trimmed and diced

1/2 pound white mushrooms, stemmed and thinly sliced

1 medium zucchini, diced

3 garlic cloves, minced

2 tablespoons chopped fresh basil

1 teaspoon chopped fresh thyme

Low-sodium soy sauce

Freshly ground black pepper

1 bunch parsley, washed and chopped

Per Serving:

128 calories

1 g total fat (7% of calories)

0 g saturated fat

0 mg cholesterol

4 g protein (13% of calories)

27 g carbohydrates (80% of calories)

6 g fiber

96 mg sodium

Makes 12 servings

1. Put the chopped tomatoes in a blender or food processor and process until smooth. Transfer to a large saucepan or stockpot and add 2 cups of stock and the barley. Simmer, stirring occasionally, for about 35 minutes, or until the barley is tender. Add more liquid, if necessary, while the barley is cooking to maintain a liquid consistency.

2. In a large sauté pan, heat the oil over medium heat. Sauté the onion, the carrot, and celery for about 5 minutes, until onion is golden. Transfer to the same stockpot with barley and add the potatoes, eggplant, mushrooms, zucchini, diced tomato, and garlic and sauté for about 5 minutes.

3. Add the remaining 4 cups stock and simmer, covered, for about 15 minutes or until the potato is tender. Stir in the basil and thyme, and add the tomato-barley mixture. Season to taste with soy sauce and pepper and ladle into heated bowls and garnish with chopped parsley.

Sun-Dried Tomato Soup with Opal Basil

I sun-dry my own tomatoes and never pack them in oil, even though we press our own olive oil at the Ranch. Oil-packed tomatoes are far higher in calories and fat than dry-packed, and frankly, our olive oil is too precious to use in that way. When necessary, I rinse the oil from store-bought oil-packed tomatoes before I use them in a recipe. So go ahead and splurge a little.

We grow many different varieties of basil, and opal basil is one of my favorites. The deep purple color and slight peppery bite add to this sumptuous soup, which can be served hot or chilled. If opal basil is not available, use what is at hand.

Per Serving:

66 calories

1 g total fat (16% of calories)

0 g saturated fat

0 mg cholesterol

3 g protein (13% of calories)

14 g carbohydrates (71% of calories)

3 g fiber

164 mg sodium

Makes 6 servings

1 teaspoon olive oil

1 medium onion, finely chopped

1 celery rib, finely chopped

3 garlic cloves, minced

4 medium tomatoes, seeded and chopped

1/2 medium all-purpose potato

2 tablespoons chopped fresh opal basil

4 cups Basic Vegetable Stock (page 75)

1/2 cup chopped sun-dried tomatoes

Salt and freshly ground black pepper

1 cup cooked brown rice

6 sprigs fresh basil, for garnish

1. In a large saucepan or stockpot, heat the oil over medium heat. Sauté the onion and celery for about 10 minutes, until the onion is golden. Add the garlic, tomatoes, potato, and basil and cook for about 2 minutes longer, until the vegetables begin to soften. Add the stock and simmer for 15 to 20 minutes, until the potato is tender.

2. Transfer the soup to a food processor and process until smooth. Return to the pot, add the sun-dried tomatoes, and simmer for about 2 minutes. Season to taste with salt and pepper and add the rice. Cook for a few minutes longer, just until the rice is heated. Serve hot or chilled, garnished with basil.

Tomato-Roasted Eggplant Soup

I "roast" diced eggplant by sautéing it quickly in a hot, dry pan. The eggplant, oregano, and orzo are the only ingredients in this soup that I don't blend in a food processor. This soup is so easy to prepare, and you'll love the garden-fresh taste.

1/2 teaspoon olive oil

1 red onion, finely chopped

1 celery rib, finely chopped

1 garlic clove, minced

8 medium tomatoes, seeded and chopped (about 2 1/2 pounds)

1/2 medium all-purpose potato

2 tablespoons chopped fresh basil

4 cups Basic Vegetable Stock (page 75)

1 round (Italian) eggplant, trimmed and diced

1 tablespoon chopped fresh oregano

1/4 cup cooked orzo

Salt and freshly ground black pepper

6 sprigs fresh oregano, for garnish

Per Serving:

106 calories

2 g total fat (12% of calories)

0 g saturated fat

0 mg cholesterol

4 g protein (13% of calories)

23 g carbohydrates (75% of calories)

6 g fiber

32 mg sodium

Makes 6 servings

1. In a large saucepan or stockpot, heat the oil over medium heat. Sauté the onion and celery for about 10 minutes, until the onion is golden. Add the garlic, tomatoes, potato, and basil and cook for about 2 minutes longer. Add the stock and simmer for 15 to 20 minutes or until the potato is tender.

2. Meanwhile, heat a large, dry sauté pan over medium-high heat and sauté the eggplant for about 5 minutes, until toasted. Set aside.

3. Transfer the ingredients in the saucepan to a food processor and blend until smooth. Return to pan and add the eggplant, oregano, and orzo. Simmer for about 2 minutes, season to taste with salt and pepper, and serve hot or chilled, garnished with sprigs of oregano.

Yellow Jubilee Tomato-Mint Soup

The gorgeous, golden-globe Yellow Jubilee tomato is a favorite of mine each summer. Look for them, or similar sweet yellow tomatoes, at farmers' markets. Of course, you can substitute other tomatoes—I suggest ripe plum tomatoes. I don't remove the peels, by the way, because I'm such a fan of the extra fiber. Sprigs of mint give this soup a great finish, served either hot or cold.

Per Serving:

65 calories

1 g total fat (10% of calories)

0 g saturated fat

0 mg cholesterol

2 g protein (12% of calories)

13 g carbohydrates (78% of calories)

1 g fiber

19 mg sodium

Makes 8 servings

1/2 teaspoon olive oil

1 medium onion, diced

1 celery rib, diced

8 medium yellow tomatoes, quartered (about 2 1/2 pounds)

1/2 medium potato or 1 small all-purpose potato, diced

3 garlic cloves, minced

3 cups Basic Vegetable Stock (page 75) or water, or more if needed

1 teaspoon chopped fresh oregano

1/4 teaspoon chopped fresh mint

1/4 teaspoon chopped fresh sage

2 tablespoons uncooked couscous

Freshly ground white pepper

Low-sodium soy sauce

8 sprigs fresh mint

1. In a large saucepan or stockpot, heat the oil over medium heat and sauté the onion and celery for about 5 minutes, until the onion is golden. Add the tomatoes, potato, and garlic and sauté for 5 minutes longer. Add the stock and simmer for about 15 minutes or until the potato is tender.

2. Transfer to a blender, add the oregano, mint, and sage and process until smooth. Return to the pot, add the couscous and more stock, if necessary, for soup to be desired thickness. Season to taste with pepper and soy sauce and simmer for about 5 minutes until the couscous is cooked. Serve garnished with mint sprigs in warm soup bowls.

Wild Mushroom Soup

Every time I make this delicious soup, I'm reminded of earlier times in my life when I'd go mushroom gathering among the redwoods of northern California with my friend, John, an expert in identification. Now the "wild" in this soup comes from shiitake, chanterelle, or oyster mushrooms—a far safer alternative than gathering your own.

1/2 teaspoon olive oil

1 medium onion, diced

1 celery rib, diced

1 pound white mushrooms, chopped

1 medium all-purpose potato, cut into 1/2-inch cubes, or 1 baked russet potato, crumbled

3 garlic cloves, chopped

1 tablespoon chopped fresh oregano

4 cups Basic Vegetable Stock (page 75), or more if needed

Low-sodium soy sauce

Freshly ground black pepper

1/4 pound shiitake, chanterelle, or oyster mushrooms, stemmed and thinly sliced

2 scallions, thinly sliced

Per Serving:

114 calories

1 g total fat (6% of calories)

0 g saturated fat

0 mg cholesterol

4 g protein (13% of calories)

23 g carbohydrates (81% of calories)

2 g fiber

16 mg sodium

Makes 8 servings

1. In a large saucepan or stockpot, heat the olive oil over medium heat and sauté the onion and celery for about 5 minutes, until the onion is golden. Add the mushrooms, potato, garlic, and oregano and sauté for about 5 minutes. Add the stock and simmer for about 15 minutes or until the potato is tender.

2. Transfer to a blender or food processor and process until smooth. Return to the pot and heat through. Adjust the consistency with stock if necessary. Season to taste with soy sauce and pepper.

3. Spray a sauté pan with vegetable oil spray and sauté the wild mushrooms over medium heat until the released juices reduce slightly. Ladle the soup into warmed bowls and garnish with the sautéed mushrooms and scallions.

Curried Carrot Soup with Dill

This is a tasty and rich soup, and even though the soup is silky smooth, no cream or any other dairy product is used. I have received great reviews when I serve this one. You will, too. Sautéed apples or raw julienned pears are a great addition to the soup.

1 teaspoon olive oil
1/2 medium onion, chopped
1 celery rib, chopped
1 green bell pepper, stemmed, seeded, and chopped
6 carrots, chopped
1 medium tomato, chopped
4 garlic cloves, minced
1 tablespoon minced fresh dill

2 tablespoons chopped fresh oregano
1 tablespoon curry powder
4 cups Basic Vegetable Stock (page 75), or more if needed
1 small zucchini, shredded
1 small carrot, shredded
Salt and freshly ground black pepper
Dill sprigs, for garnish

Per Serving:

71 calories

1 g total fat (15% of calories)

0 g saturated fat

0 mg cholesterol

2 g protein (10% of calories)

15 g carbohydrates (75% of calories)

4 g fiber

92 mg sodium

Makes 6 servings

1. In a stockpot, heat the oil over medium heat and sauté the onion, celery, and bell pepper for about 10 minutes, until the onion is golden. Add the carrot, tomato, garlic, dill, and oregano and cook for 6 or 7 minutes, stirring, until the tomato softens. Add the curry powder and stock, and simmer for about 20 minutes or until the carrots are soft.

2. Transfer the soup to a blender or food processor and blend until smooth (this may have to be done in batches). Return to the pot and add the shredded zucchini and carrot. Simmer for about 2 minutes. Season to taste with salt and pepper. Serve hot or chilled, garnished with dill.

Broccoli Soup

Potatoes, broccoli, and other vegetables are simmered and then blended to create this smooth soup. Just before serving, the soup is garnished with crunchy broccoli or cauliflower florets.

1/2 teaspoon olive oil

1 medium onion, diced

1 carrot, diced

1 celery rib, diced

2 1/2 pounds broccoli, cut into florets

1 small all-purpose potato, diced

3 garlic cloves, chopped

4 cups Basic Vegetable Stock (page 75) or water

1 tablespoon chopped fresh oregano

Low-sodium soy sauce

Freshly ground black pepper

1 tablespoon uncooked couscous

2 scallions, thinly sliced

Per Serving:

65 calories

1 g total fat (8% of calories)

0 g saturated fat

0 mg cholesterol

3 g protein (19% of calories)

12 g carbohydrates (73% of calories)

1 g fiber

32 mg sodium

Makes 8 servings

1. In a large saucepan or stockpot, heat the olive oil over medium heat and sauté the onion, carrot, and celery for about 5 minutes, until the onion is golden. Add all but 1 1/2 cups of the broccoli, potato, and garlic and sauté for 5 minutes longer. Add the stock and simmer for about 15 minutes or until the broccoli and potato are tender.

2. Transfer to a blender or food processor, add the oregano, and process until nearly smooth. If the broccoli is fibrous, strain the puree through a sieve and discard the pulp.

3. Return the soup to the pan and heat through. Season to taste with soy sauce and black pepper. Add the reserved florets and the couscous, and simmer for about 5 minutes, or until the broccoli is tender and couscous is cooked through. Ladle into heated bowls and garnish with sliced scallions.

Taking the Ranch Home

Breathe! Who needs to be reminded? But you *do* need to remind yourself to take *big* breaths—belly breaths—from the bottom of the lungs. Push away from what you're doing if you have a sedentary job and take big gulps of air. Refresh yourself. Deep breathing brings more oxygen to the brain, and it can't help but put you into the present, making you *mindful* of the body at a most fundamental level.

Butternut Squash Soup

You'll be surprised by this soup's smoothness, despite its not having a drop of cream. Oven-roasting the squash gives it a smoky flavor that makes me think of my Colorado childhood. I'd sit in my grandma's toasty kitchen, eating a bowl of warm homemade soup and watching the flying snow blanket the fenced fields. To this day, this soup takes me home.

3 1/2 to 4 pounds butternut squash (2 medium squash)

1 medium all-purpose potato

1/2 teaspoon olive oil

1 medium onion, diced

1 carrot, diced

1 celery rib, diced

3 garlic cloves, minced

1 tablespoon chopped fresh oregano

1 teaspoon chopped fresh thyme

4 cups Basic Vegetable Stock (page 75) or water, or more if needed

Low-sodium soy sauce

Freshly ground black pepper

2 scallions, thinly sliced

Per Serving:

125 calories

0 g total fat (4% of calories)

0 g saturated fat

0 mg cholesterol

3 g protein (9% of calories)

27 g carbohydrates (87% of calories)

3 g fiber

20 mg sodium

Makes 10 servings

1. Preheat the oven to 350°F.

2. Split the butternut squash in half lengthwise, scoop out the seeds, and place peel side down in a shallow baking pan. Bake for about 1 hour or until soft and golden. Bake the potato at the same time until fork-tender. Let cool. Peel the cooled squash and potato and cut into small pieces. Set aside.

3. In a large saucepan or stockpot, heat the oil over medium heat and sauté the onion, carrot, and celery for about 5 minutes, until the onion is golden. Add the garlic, oregano, thyme, squash, and potato and cook for about 5 minutes. Add the stock and simmer for about 15 minutes.

4. Transfer to a blender or food processor and process until smooth. Return to the pan and heat through. Adjust the consistency with additional broth, if necessary, and season to taste with soy sauce and black pepper. Ladle into soup bowls and garnish with scallions.

Cauliflower Soup

Grainy mustard lends some bite and vinegary tartness to an otherwise bland, but smooth and creamy soup. Serve with lime wedges for another hit of flavor.

Per Serving:

51 calories

0 g total fat (9% of calories)

0 g saturated fat

0 mg cholesterol

2 g protein (15% of calories)

10 g carbohydrates (76% of calories)

1 g fiber

40 mg sodium

Makes 8 servings

1 head of cauliflower, trimmed and cut into florets (about 1 pound)

1/2 teaspoon olive oil

1 medium onion, diced

1 carrot, sliced into 1/4-inch rounds

1 celery rib, diced

1 small all-purpose potato, peeled and diced

3 garlic cloves, minced

4 cups Basic Vegetable Stock (page 75) or water, or more if needed

1 teaspoon coarse-grain Dijon mustard

1 tablespoon chopped fresh oregano or basil

Low-sodium soy sauce

Freshly ground black pepper

1 tablespoon uncooked couscous (optional)

2 bunches spinach washed, julienned and steamed

1 lime, quartered (optional)

1. Set aside 1 cup of cauliflower florets. Coarsely chop the remaining florets.

2. Heat the oil in a large saucepan or stockpot over medium heat and sauté the onion, carrot, and celery for about 5 minutes, until the onion is golden. Add the cauliflower, potato, and garlic and sauté for 5 minutes. Add the stock and mustard, and simmer for about 15 minutes, until the cauliflower is tender.

3. Transfer to a blender or food processor, add the oregano or basil, and process until smooth. Return to the pot and heat through. Adjust the consistency with additional broth or water, if necessary. Season to taste with soy sauce and pepper.

4. Add the couscous, if desired, and the reserved florets and simmer for about 8 minutes or until the florets are tender and the couscous is cooked. Top with the spinach and lime quarters.

Spinach Soup

I add a tablespoon of couscous in the final stages of preparing some of my soups because I like the added texture, and it helps to thicken a soup while only slightly increasing the calories (with no added fat). A garnish of sautéed shiitake mushrooms and scallions tops this one off.

Per Serving:

85 calories

1 g total fat (7% of calories)

0 g saturated fat

0 mg cholesterol

3 g protein (13% of calories)

19 g carbohydrates (80% of calories)

4 g fiber

108 mg sodium

Makes 8 servings

1/2 teaspoon olive oil

1 medium onion, diced

1 carrot, diced

1 celery rib, diced

2 pounds spinach (about 3 bunches), leaves only, washed well

1 medium all-purpose potato, finely diced

3 garlic cloves, chopped

4 cups Basic Vegetable Stock (page 75) or water, or more if needed

1 tablespoon chopped fresh oregano

1 teaspoon chopped fresh sage

Low-sodium soy sauce

Freshly ground black pepper

1 tablespoon uncooked couscous

1/4 pound shiitake mushrooms, stemmed and thinly sliced

2 scallions, thinly sliced

1. In a large saucepan or stockpot, heat the oil over medium heat and sauté the onion, carrot, and celery for about 5 minutes, until the onion is golden. Add the spinach, potato, and garlic and cook for 5 minutes longer. Add the stock and simmer for about 5 minutes or until the potato is soft.

2. Transfer to a blender or food processor, add the oregano and sage, and process until smooth. Return to the pot, add more stock or water to adjust the consistency, if necessary, and heat through. Season with soy sauce and pepper. Stir in the couscous and simmer for about 5 minutes, until couscous is cooked.

3. Spray a small sauté pan with vegetable oil spray. Sauté the mushrooms over medium heat for about 5 minutes, until soft.

4. Ladle the soup into bowls and garnish with sautéed mushrooms and sliced scallions.

Potato-Corn Soup with Chipotle-Cilantro Pesto

This is a cocina *(kitchen) staff favorite when the first harvests of our fresh garden corn arrive in the kitchen. I love this soup with the pesto and a little squeeze of lime.*

1 teaspoon olive oil

1 medium onion, chopped

1 celery rib, chopped

1 carrot, chopped

1 medium all-purpose potato, chopped

1 red and 1 yellow bell pepper, stemmed, seeded, and chopped

1 garlic clove, chopped

1 jalapeño pepper, quartered

2 tablespoons chopped fresh oregano

1 medium zucchini, sliced

1 medium yellow summer squash, sliced

1 1/2 quarts Basic Vegetable Stock (page 75)

1 cup corn kernels

Salt and freshly ground black pepper

2 tablespoons Chipotle-Cilantro Pesto (page 95) (optional)

1. In a large saucepan over medium-high heat, heat the oil and sauté the onion, celery, carrot, and potato until the onion is golden, 5 to 6 minutes. Add the bell peppers, garlic, jalapeño, oregano, and squash, and sauté 2 minutes. Add the stock and simmer 5 minutes.

2. Sieve half of the cooked vegetables from the stock (remove jalapeño if you wish) and place in a food processor, then pulse 10 seconds to lightly puree. Add the puree to the saucepan and stir in the corn. Simmer 10 minutes. Season to taste. Serve garnished with pesto, if desired.

Per Serving:

73 calories

2 g total fat (21% of calories)

0 g saturated fat

0 mg cholesterol

2 g protein (12% of calories)

14 g carbohydrates (69% of calories)

3 g fiber

119 mg sodium

Makes 8 servings

Chipotle-Cilantro Pesto

This is a great pesto and an especially interesting one because it is made with chipotle chiles packed in adobo sauce. If you are a chile lover, add more chile, but if you are still using your chile training wheels, you may want to cut back a little or use the adobo sauce only, which is less fiery than the chile itself. For further flavor enhancement, add tarragon, rosemary, sun-dried tomatoes, roasted red bell peppers, roasted eggplant...you name it! All are great additions. Experiment.

2 cups chopped fresh spinach leaves

2 cups chopped fresh cilantro

1/4 cup chopped flat-leaf parsley

1/4 cup toasted shelled pumpkin seeds

2 tablespoons grated Parmesan cheese

1 tablespoon chopped fresh oregano

3 cloves garlic

1 chipotle chile in adobo sauce

1 tablespoon plus 1 teaspoon olive oil

1 tablespoon lime juice

In a food processor, combine the spinach, cilantro, parsley, pumpkin seeds, cheese, oregano, garlic, and chile and pulse to blend. With the motor running, add the olive oil and lime juice and process for 15 or 20 minutes until blended. Scrape into a container, cover, and refrigerate until ready to use. The pesto keeps for 3 or 4 days in the refrigerator.

Per Teaspoon:

28 calories

1 g total fat (42% of calories)

0 g saturated fat

3 mg cholesterol

1 g protein (18% of calories)

3 g carbohydrates (40% of calories)

1 g fiber

24 mg sodium

Makes about 2 cups

NOTE: *Chipotle chiles packed in adobo sauce are sold canned in many supermarkets and specialty shops.*

Roasted Red Pepper Soup with Couscous

With summer comes wonderful bell peppers. This soup has great taste, almost no fat, and only 60 calories. Dig in! The smoky flavor from the roasted peppers and the fragrance of the fresh thyme make this one of the best I make. It's also very good chilled on a warm day.

1/2 teaspoon olive oil
1/2 medium onion, chopped
1/2 carrot, chopped
1 celery rib, chopped
4 garlic cloves, chopped
1/2 medium all-purpose potato
3 roasted red bell peppers
  (pages 58–59)
3 roasted green bell peppers
  (pages 58–59)

4 cups Basic Vegetable Stock
  (page 75)
1 teaspoon chopped fresh oregano
1/2 teaspoon chopped fresh thyme
Salt and freshly ground black pepper
2 tablespoons uncooked couscous
  (see Note)
Sprigs of fresh thyme, for garnish

Per Serving:

64 calories

1 g total fat (9% of calories)

0 g saturated fat

0 mg cholesterol

2 g protein (12% of calories)

14 g carbohydrates (79% of calories)

3 g fiber

64 mg sodium

Makes 6 servings

NOTE: *If you are going to serve this soup chilled, omit the couscous.*

1. In a large saucepan, heat the oil over medium heat and sauté the onion, carrot, and celery for 5 or 6 minutes, until the onion is golden. Add the garlic, potato, and roasted peppers and cook an additional 5 minutes, stirring. Add the stock and simmer, covered, for about 15 minutes or until the potato is tender.

2. Transfer to a food processor and add the oregano and thyme. (Take care because the soup with be hot!) Puree for about 10 seconds, until the vegetables are still chunky. Return to the pan and bring to a simmer. Season to taste with salt and pepper and add the couscous. Cook for about 2 minutes, until the couscous is cooked. Ladle into bowls and garnish with thyme sprigs.

Mexican Corn Soup

When the season's first corn arrives fresh from the garden, you can bet that it will be on the menu that day. Grilling the corn adds a deep, roasted corn flavor. I like to place a dollop of Chipotle-Cilantro Pesto (page 95) atop this soup.

1/2 teaspoon olive oil

1 medium onion, diced

1 celery rib, diced

1 small all-purpose potato, diced

2 garlic cloves, chopped

4 cups Basic Vegetable Stock (page 75)

3 cups fresh corn kernels (from 3 or 4 ears of corn)

1 tablespoon chopped fresh oregano

Low-sodium soy sauce

Freshly ground black pepper

1 ear of corn, roasted and kernels cut off (see Note)

1. In a large saucepan or stockpot, heat the oil over medium heat and sauté the onion and celery for about 5 minutes, until the onion is golden. Add the potato and garlic, and sauté for 5 minutes longer. Add the stock and simmer for about 10 minutes or until the potato is tender. Add the corn kernels and cook for 5 minutes more, until the corn is tender.

2. Transfer to a blender or food processor, add the oregano, and process until smooth. Return to the pot and heat through. Season to taste with soy sauce and pepper. Ladle into heated bowls and garnish with roasted corn kernels.

Per Serving:

83 calories

1 g total fat (10% of calories)

0 g saturated fat

0 mg cholesterol

2 g protein (12% of calories)

16 g carbohydrates (78% of calories)

1 g fiber

16 mg sodium

Makes 10 servings

NOTE: *To roast an ear of corn, place the husked corn over an open flame or hot grill, or under a broiler, and cook, turning, until golden brown—taking care not to burn the kernels. Roast more ears and add the extra kernels to the soup if you like a particularly smoky corn flavor.*

Black Bean Soup

In my previous culinary life as a chef cooking French and California high-calorie food, I used to make Cajun black bean soup with andouille sausage and chicken. It was very good, but loaded with fat and calories and more than 28 mg of cholesterol. Now that I've "seen the light," I make a low-fat, low-cholesterol—but equally delicious—meatless version. Always cook beans at a medium, moving simmer and always keep them covered with at least two inches of water or stock to ensure even cooking.

BEANS

1 medium onion, diced

2 garlic cloves, minced

1 tablespoon chopped fresh oregano

1 cup black beans, soaked overnight in water to cover, and drained

1 teaspoon ground cumin

1 teaspoon low-sodium soy sauce

8 cups Basic Vegetable Stock (page 75) or water, or more if needed

Freshly ground black pepper

SOUP

1/2 teaspoon olive oil

1 medium onion, diced

1 celery rib, diced

2 red or yellow bell peppers, stemmed, seeded, and diced

1 medium tomato, diced

4 ounces shiitake mushrooms, stemmed and sliced

2 garlic cloves, minced

1 jalapeño pepper, seeded and minced

2 teaspoons ground cumin

1 tablespoon chopped fresh oregano

Low-sodium soy sauce

Freshly ground black pepper

1/4 cup nonfat plain yogurt

1/4 cup chopped fresh cilantro

1 scallion, both green and white parts, thinly sliced

Per Serving:

144 calories

1 g total fat (7% of calories)

0 g saturated fat

0 mg cholesterol

8 g protein (20% of calories)

28 g carbohydrates (73% of calories)

6 g fiber

225 mg sodium

Makes 8 servings

1. To prepare the beans, lightly spray a large saucepan or stockpot with vegetable oil spray. Sauté the onion, garlic, and oregano over medium heat for about 5 minutes, until the onion is golden. Add the beans, cumin, soy sauce, and stock. Bring to a boil, reduce the heat, and simmer for about 1 1/2 hours, until beans are very soft. Take care that the beans are covered with stock or water during cooking. Set the pot aside.

2. To make the soup, in a large sauté pan, heat the olive oil over medium heat and sauté the onion, celery, and bell peppers for about 5 minutes, until the onion is golden. Add the tomato, mushrooms, garlic, jalapeño, cumin, and oregano and sauté for 2 to 3 minutes.

3. Add the vegetables to the beans and simmer over medium heat for about 5 minutes. Season to taste with soy sauce and pepper and add more stock or water to adjust the consistency.

4. Ladle the soup into heated bowls and garnish each with a dollop of yogurt, some cilantro, and some scallion slices.

White Bean and Eggplant Soup

This popular soup is hearty and flavorful. I like to combine a piece of baked potato and half a cup of soup in the blender for three or four seconds to give it a thick, chunky consistency. You're going to like this one—and it's even better the next day!

BEANS

4 cups Basic Vegetable Stock (page 75)

1/2 cup dried white beans, soaked overnight in water to cover, and drained

2 garlic cloves, minced

1 teaspoon salt (optional)

1/4 teaspoon freshly ground black pepper

SOUP

1/2 teaspoon olive oil

1/2 cup chopped onion

1/2 cup chopped carrot

1/2 chopped celery

1/2 cup chopped zucchini

2 garlic cloves, chopped

1/2 cup diced tomato

1/2 cup cubed eggplant

1 tablespoon chopped fresh oregano

1/4 teaspoon chopped fresh rosemary

2 cups Basic Vegetable Stock (page 75), or more if needed

Low-sodium soy sauce

Freshly ground black pepper

Per Serving:

69 calories

1 g total fat (8% of calories)

0 g saturated fat

0 mg cholesterol

4 g protein (21% of calories)

13g carbohydrates (71% of calories)

4 g fiber

323 mg sodium

Makes 6 servings

1. To prepare the beans, put the stock, beans, garlic, salt, and pepper in a large saucepan or stockpot, bring to a simmer over medium heat, and cook for about 1 hour, until the beans are tender when pinched between thumb and forefinger. Take care that the beans are covered with stock or water during cooking. Set the pot aside.

2. To make the soup, in a medium sauté pan, heat the olive oil over medium heat and sauté the onion, carrot, and celery for about 5 minutes. Add the zucchini, garlic, tomato, and eggplant and sauté for about 5 minutes longer, until the eggplant begins to soften. Add to the beans and stir in the herbs. Add the stock or water to adjust the consistency. Season to taste with the soy sauce and pepper, and simmer for 5 to 8 minutes to bring the flavors together. Ladle into soup bowls and serve.

Yellow Split Pea Soup with Swiss Chard

Split peas require no soaking and cook in less than 45 minutes, so this beautiful, warming soup is fast and easy to make. Green split peas can be substituted, but the soup won't be as pretty.

PEAS

1 medium onion, diced

2 garlic cloves, minced

1 tablespoon chopped fresh oregano, or 1 teaspoon dried

1 cup split yellow peas, sorted and rinsed

1 teaspoon low-sodium soy sauce

Freshly ground black pepper

4 cups Basic Vegetable Stock (page 75) or water, or more if needed

SOUP

1/2 teaspoon olive oil

1 medium onion, diced

2 red or yellow bell peppers, stemmed, seeded, and diced

1 celery rib, diced

1 medium tomato, diced

1/4 pound oyster mushrooms, stemmed and sliced

1 garlic clove, minced

1 tablespoon chopped fresh oregano

Low-sodium soy sauce

Freshly ground black pepper

1 large leaf Swiss chard, julienned

Per Serving:

94 calories

1 g total fat (7% of calories)

0 g saturated fat

0 mg cholesterol

6 g protein (23% of calories)

16 g carbohydrates (70% of calories)

7 g fiber

192 mg sodium

Makes 10 servings

1. To prepare the peas, lightly spray a large saucepan or stockpot with vegetable oil spray and sauté the onion, garlic, and oregano over medium heat for about 5 minutes until the onion is golden. Add the peas, soy sauce, pepper to taste, and stock. Bring to a boil over high heat, reduce the heat, and simmer slowly 45 minutes, or until the peas are very soft. Take care that the peas are covered with stock or water during cooking. Set the pot aside.

2. To prepare the soup, in a large sauté pan, heat the oil over medium heat and sauté the onion, bell pepper, and celery for about 5 minutes, or until the onion is golden. Add the tomato, mushrooms, and garlic and sauté for 2 to 3 minutes. Stir the vegetables into the cooked peas and add the oregano, soy sauce, and black pepper; simmer for about 5 minutes. Add the Swiss chard and more stock or water, if necessary, for consistency. Heat for a minute or two and ladle into heated bowls and serve.

Curried Lentil Soup

The meatiness of lentils, earthy shiitakes, Indian curry, and the fresh bite of tomatoes and scallions all come together in this soup. Don't be discouraged by the lengthy ingredient list; I still consider this a fairly quick, easy-to-make soup. Lentils will cook in just 25 to 35 minutes, and while they simmer you can assemble the other ingredients. Serve this soup on the same day it's prepared, but all its flavors will come together even more if refrigerated and then reheated.

Per Serving:

126 calories

1 g total fat (9% of calories)

0 g saturated fat

0 mg cholesterol

6 g protein (18% of calories)

26 g carbohydrates (73% of calories)

8 g fiber

209 mg sodium

Makes 8 servings

LENTILS

1/2 teaspoon olive oil

1 medium onion, diced

1 garlic clove, minced

1 tablespoon chopped fresh thyme

1/2 cup lentils, rinsed

1 teaspoon curry powder

Pinch of freshly ground black pepper

1 tablespoon low-sodium soy sauce

3 cups Basic Vegetable Stock (page 75) or water, or more if needed

VEGETABLES

1/2 teaspoon olive oil

1 medium onion, diced

1 celery rib, diced

1 red or yellow bell pepper, stemmed, seeded, and diced

1 medium tomato, diced

1/4 pound shiitake mushrooms, stemmed and thinly sliced

3 garlic cloves, minced

1 tablespoon chopped fresh oregano

1 teaspoon low-sodium soy sauce, or to taste

SALSA
1 medium tomato, diced
2 scallions, thinly sliced
1 teaspoon chopped fresh thyme

1. To prepare the lentils, in a large saucepan or stockpot, heat the oil over medium heat and sauté the onion, garlic, and thyme for about 5 minutes, until the onion is golden. Add the lentils, curry powder, pepper, soy sauce, and stock. Bring to a boil, reduce the heat, and simmer for about 45 minutes or until the lentils are al dente. Take care that the lentils are covered with stock or water during cooking. Set the pot aside.

2. To prepare the vegetables, in a sauté pan, heat the oil over medium heat and sauté the onion, celery, and pepper for about 5 minutes, or until the onion is golden. Add the tomato, mushrooms, garlic, and oregano and sauté for 2 or 3 minutes. Add to the lentils and simmer for about 5 minutes until blended. Adjust seasoning with soy sauce. Add more vegetable broth or water if the consistency is too thick.

3. To prepare the salsa, in a small bowl combine the tomato, scallions, and thyme and mix gently. Ladle the soup into warmed soup bowls and garnish each with 2 tablespoons of salsa.

Salads and Dressings

I CAN MAKE A MEAL *out of a fresh green salad, but you have to pick the freshest of the fresh—nothing wilted or sagging. Remember, some greens such as arugula bring flavor, while others such as romaine, provide texture.*

The natural flavors of fresh vegetables and lettuces straight from our Ranch gardens are delicious enough, but I especially love them with my full-flavored creamy salad dressing. It's teeming with herbaceous, garlicky flavors but still low in calories and fat.

Many of my dressings go far beyond the green salad realm: they're great over steamed vegetables, rice, or pastas, or you can use them as marinades. My favorite option? The blue cheese dressing over a saffron-stuffed baked potato.

All my dressings are very, very low in calories, and with the exception of one or two that have a scant gram of fat per serving, all are nonfat. I try to keep a dressing recipe fast and easy to make. Meant to be used fresh on the freshest produce you can find, they won't keep more than three to four days in the refrigerator. But you'll enjoy them long before that, anyway, no?

Tres Estrellas Salad

Tres Estrellas, meaning three stars, is the name of Rancho La Puerta's six-acre organic garden where I have the pleasure of harvesting a wonderful bounty of vegetables, herbs, fruits, and flowers, all of which grow to be healthy, delicious, and free of any herbicides or pesticides. This salad is named in honor of the garden and is a mouthwatering array of colorful lettuces and seasonal just-picked vegetables, with edible flowers adorning the plate. Start with a mix of greens and lettuces as a base, add your favorite herbs, and then toss in fresh vegetables. Be sure to tear, rather than cut, the greens.

1 head green leaf lettuce
1 cup radicchio leaves
1 cup chopped beet greens
1/2 cup arugula leaves
1/2 cup mâche
1/2 cup chopped fresh flat-leaf parsley
1/2 cup fresh basil leaves
1 small zucchini, cut into 2-inch julienne
1 carrot, cut into 2-inch julienne
1 red bell pepper, stemmed, seeded, and cut into 2-inch julienne

1/2 cup broccoli florets
1 beet, cooked, peeled, and cut into 2-inch julienne
1 scallion, thinly sliced
3 medium tomatoes, quartered
24 fresh edible flowers, such as johnny jump-ups or pansies
Herbed Yogurt Nonfat Dressing (page 149), Papaya-Lime Dressing (page 146), or other nonfat dressing

Per Serving (without dressing):
125 calories
2 g total fat (10% of calories)
0 g saturated fat
0 mg cholesterol
7 g protein (18% of calories)
27 g carbohydrates (72% of calories)
10 g fiber
114 mg sodium
Makes 6 servings

1. In a large bowl, toss the lettuce, radicchio, beet greens, arugula, mâche, parsley, and basil; cover with a moist towel and refrigerate.

2. Toss the zucchini, carrot, red pepper, broccoli, beet, and scallion with the greens. Spoon on chilled plates. Arrange the tomatoes around the greens and garnish with the flowers. Top with your choice of dressing.

Mixed Greens with Tomatoes and Feta

I'm in heaven every summer, when the sun starts warming our tomato and basil plants—row after row of them. Their daily growth is almost visible. Just give me some warm, fresh-baked French bread to eat with this salad and I'm a happy person.

1/4 cup balsamic vinegar
1/2 teaspoon extra-virgin olive oil
2 tablespoons chopped fresh basil
4 garlic cloves, minced
Freshly ground black pepper
1 head radicchio, leaves torn into
   bite-size pieces

1 cup torn arugula leaves
1 cup torn red leaf lettuce
1 cup torn Bibb lettuce
1 cup mâche
4 to 6 tomatoes, quartered
3 tablespoons crumbled feta cheese
4 sprigs fresh basil

Per Serving:
54 calories
2 g total fat (30% of calories)
1 g saturated fat
3 mg cholesterol
2 g protein (16% of calories)
8 g carbohydrates (56% of calories)
1 g fiber
65 mg sodium
Makes 4 servings

1. In a small mixing bowl, combine the vinegar, olive oil, basil, garlic, and pepper to taste, and whisk well.

2. In a large bowl, mix all the torn greens, reserving 4 outer radicchio leaves.

3. Center one of the reserved radicchio leaves on each plate and top each with 2 cups of the greens. Arrange the tomato quarters around the greens and drizzle vinaigrette over the greens. Sprinkle with feta and garnish with a basil sprig.

Arugula, Mâche, Radicchio, and Pears with Balsamic Vinegar

In the fall and winter, I am lucky to have an abundance of both lettuce varieties and pears, which is how I came to develop this salad. The pears and balsamic vinegar just seem to be made for each another, and the arugula's peppery bite sets the salad off. I sometimes compromise the fat and calorie count by adding a few toasted walnuts to top the salad off. If you can't find arugula or radicchio, use other bitter greens, such as dandelion or mustard.

2 tablespoons balsamic vinegar

1/2 teaspoon extra-virgin olive oil

1 garlic clove, minced

1 tablespoon chopped fresh basil

Freshly ground black pepper

4 cups torn arugula leaves

4 cups mâche

4 radicchio leaves

2 Bosc pears, cored and quartered

2 tablespoons crumbled feta cheese

1. In a small bowl, combine the vinegar, 2 tablespoons water, the oil, garlic, basil and pepper to taste, and whisk well. Set aside to let the flavors marry.

2. In a large mixing bowl, toss the arugula and mâche together. Center a radicchio leaf on each of 4 chilled plates and top with the greens. Arrange the pear quarters around the greens and drizzle the vinaigrette over the salads. Sprinkle the feta cheese over the top and serve immediately.

Per Serving:

151 calories

3 g total fat (16% of calories)

1 g saturated fat

3 mg cholesterol

6 g protein (16% of calories)

26 g carbohydrates (68% of calories)

4 g fiber

159 mg sodium

Makes 4 servings

Taking the Ranch Home

Bait and switch: Thirty years ago Rancho La Puerta founder Deborah Szekely started playfully advocating a little anarchy in the tablesetting department at home. Her scheme? Switch the use of your dishware. Serve a big, delicious salad on a dinner plate. Then serve the entree on a salad plate. Use the smallest dish you have for dessert. Even a small scoop of sorbet will look bigger in a small dish, especially if you eat it with a demitasse spoon.

Sesame Broccoli Stir-Fry Salad

Black, rather than the usual white, sesame seeds set off the other vibrant colors of this pretty dish. As a salad, this preparation is very low in calories and fat. To make it a main dish, substitute half a pound of cooked cellophane noodles for the lettuce, adding 200 calories and .5 grams of fat per serving. As with any stir-fry, you'll need to work very fast, so have all ingredients prepared, measured, and at the ready.

Juice of 2 limes

2 tablespoons coarsely chopped fresh ginger and 1 teaspoon minced

2 cups broccoli florets

1/4 cup Basic Vegetable Stock (page 75) or water

1 teaspoon cornstarch

1/2 teaspoon Asian sesame oil

4 garlic cloves, sliced

2 scallions, sliced

1 cup stemmed and thinly sliced shiitake mushrooms

1 red bell pepper, stemmed, seeded, and cut into 2-inch julienne

1/2 carrot, cut into 1/2-inch-thick slices

1/2 toasted chile de arbol, stemmed, seeded, and chopped (page 57)

1/4 cup low-sodium soy sauce

3 tablespoons mirin (see Note)

2 tablespoons rice vinegar

4 cups shredded romaine lettuce

1 teaspoon black sesame seeds (see Note)

Per Serving:

142 calories

2 g total fat (10% of calories)

0 g saturated fat

0 mg cholesterol

8 g protein (18% of calories)

31 g carbohydrates (72% of calories)

8 g fiber

867 mg sodium

Makes 4 servings

NOTE: *Mirin, or sweet Japanese wine, and black sesame seeds are available in supermarkets and Asian markets.*

1. Fill a large saucepan with water. Add the lime juice and coarsely chopped ginger and bring to a boil over high heat. Add the broccoli and cook for about 30 seconds, until the broccoli turns bright green. Drain, rinse the broccoli under cold running water to stop the cooking, and set aside.

2. In a small bowl, whisk together the stock and cornstarch until the cornstarch dissolves.

3. In a large sauté pan, heat the sesame oil over medium heat. Add the garlic, remaining minced ginger, scallions, mushrooms, bell pepper, and carrot and stir-fry for about 2 minutes, until the vegetables begin to soften. Add the chile, soy sauce, mirin, and vinegar and stir-fry for 2 minutes longer. Whisk again and then add the stock-cornstarch mixture to the vegetables and simmer for about 30 seconds to thicken. Add the broccoli and stir-fry for about 1 minute until heated through.

4. Divide the lettuce among 4 plates and top with the stir-fried vegetables. Garnish with a pinch of sesame seeds and serve.

Broccoli Tofu Salad with Toasted Sesame Seeds

This is a great salad with tons of nutritional benefits and very little fat and calories. The day before making it, let the tofu drain for at least four hours, and then marinate it overnight in the refrigerator to get the most flavor.

1/2 pound tofu, firm, drained (pages 186–187)
1 cup Asian Marinade (page 35)
Juice of 2 limes
2 tablespoons chopped fresh ginger and 1 teaspoon minced
2 cups broccoli florets
1/2 teaspoon Asian sesame oil
4 garlic cloves, sliced
2 scallions, thinly sliced
1 cup stemmed and thinly sliced shiitake mushrooms
1 red bell pepper, stemmed, seeded, and cut into 2-inch julienne
1/2 carrot, thinly sliced
1/2 chile de arbol, toasted (page 57)
2 tablespoons low-sodium soy sauce
1/4 cup rice vinegar
4 cups shredded romaine lettuce
1 teaspoon toasted sesame seeds

Per Serving:

208 calories
6 g total fat (23% of calories)
1 g saturated fat
0 mg cholesterol
14 g protein (22% of calories)
34 g carbohydrates (55% of calories)
9 g fiber
707 mg sodium

Makes 4 servings

1. Place the tofu in a bowl, top with the marinade, turn several times to coat, cover, and refrigerate for at least 1 hour. (The longer the tofu marinates, the more flavor it develops.)

2. Preheat the oven to 375°F. Lightly spray a baking sheet with vegetable oil spray.

3. Lift the tofu from the marinade and cut it into 1-inch-thick cubes. Lay the tofu cubes in a single layer on the baking sheet and bake for 15 to 20 minutes, until cubes are golden. Set aside to cool.

4. Fill a 2-quart saucepan with water, add the lime juice and chopped ginger, and bring to a boil over high heat. Add the broccoli and blanch for about 30 seconds, until bright green. Drain and cool under cold running water and set aside.

5. In a large sauté pan, heat the sesame oil over medium heat and sauté the garlic, remaining minced ginger, scallions, and mushrooms for about 1 minute, tossing. Add the pepper, carrot, chile, soy sauce, and vinegar and stir-fry for about 3 minutes, until the pepper and carrot start to soften and the mixture is fragrant. Add the broccoli and toss for about 1 minute longer, until the broccoli is hot. Add the tofu and stir-fry for about 1 minute, just to mix.

6. Arrange 1 cup of the lettuce in the center of each plate and top with equal portions of the vegetables and tofu. Top with toasted sesame seeds.

Jicama, Red Onion, and Orange Salad

Jicama is a tropical tuber. Mexicans and Latinos like to feast on slices as an appetizer with some wedges of lime or orange squeezed over them. Here it's used in a refreshing, crunchy salad—a Ranch guest favorite.

1/4 cup balsamic vinegar
2 garlic cloves, minced
1 teaspoon chopped fresh oregano
Pinch of freshly ground black pepper
4 navel oranges
1 head romaine lettuce, torn into pieces
1 jicama, peeled and cut into 2 1/2-inch-long slices
1 red onion, thinly sliced
Oregano sprigs, for garnish

Per Serving:

98 calories

0 g total fat (3% of calories)

0 g saturated fat

0 mg cholesterol

3 g protein (10% of calories)

21 g carbohydrates (87% of calories)

2 g fiber

4 mg sodium

Makes 6 servings

1. In a small mixing bowl, combine the vinegar, garlic, oregano, and black pepper and whisk to mix.

2. Holding the oranges over the bowl, peel and cut away the outside membrane. Using a sharp knife, separate the orange segments, letting the juices collect in the bowl, and drop the segments into the bowl as they are separated.

3. To serve, arrange the lettuce on chilled plates. Top with jicama and red onion and arrange the orange segments over the salad. Garnish with a sprig of oregano and serve the dressing on the side.

Spinach and Red Onion Salad

Citrus, onion, and spinach—a classic salad combination. Sprigs of fresh herbs are what make an out-of-the-ordinary salad, along with a tablespoon of chopped orange zest, orange or grapefruit juice, and a squeeze of lime. Hard-cooked egg whites give it a protein boost.

Per Serving:

67 calories

2 g total fat (28% of calories)

1 g saturated fat

71 mg cholesterol

4 g protein (22% of calories)

9 g carbohydrates (50% of calories)

2 g fiber

50 mg sodium

Makes 6 servings

1/2 red onion, thinly sliced

1 teaspoon fresh lime juice

1/3 cup fresh orange or grapefruit juice

1/4 cup red wine vinegar

1 shallot, minced

1 garlic clove, minced

1 tablespoon chopped orange zest

1/2 teaspoon chopped fresh basil

1/2 teaspoon chopped fresh cilantro

1/2 teaspoon chopped fresh oregano

1/2 teaspoon chopped fresh thyme

Freshly ground black pepper

12 cups spinach leaves, well washed (about 1 1/2 pounds)

1 head radicchio, separated into leaves

2 large hard-cooked egg whites, chopped

1 carrot, grated

6 sprigs fresh cilantro

6 sprigs fresh basil

6 sprigs fresh oregano

6 sprigs fresh thyme

1. In a small bowl, toss the onion and lime juice and set aside.

2. In another small bowl, mix the orange juice, vinegar, shallot, garlic, orange zest, chopped herbs, and black pepper to taste.

3. Put the spinach and radicchio in a bowl and add the egg whites, carrot, and marinated onion. Drizzle with vinaigrette and toss well. Serve on chilled plates, garnished with herb sprigs.

Spinach-Radicchio Salad with Enoki Mushrooms

Radicchio, a member of the chicory family (others include curly endive and escarole), adds its bitter flavor to this spinach salad.

1/2 red onion, thinly sliced

1 red bell pepper, stemmed, seeded, and cut into 2-inch julienne

1 yellow bell pepper, stemmed, seeded, and cut into 2-inch julienne

1 teaspoon fresh lime juice

1 teaspoon extra-virgin olive oil

1/3 cup fresh orange or lemon juice

3 tablespoons balsamic vinegar

2 garlic cloves, minced

1 scallion, thinly sliced

1 teaspoon chopped fresh thyme

Freshly ground black pepper

8 cups spinach leaves, well washed (about 1 pound)

1/2 head radicchio, 6 outside leaves reserved and rest julienned

1 ounce enoki mushrooms, ends trimmed

6 sprigs fresh thyme

Per Serving:

35 calories

1 g total fat (23% of calories)

0 g saturated fat

0 mg cholesterol

2% protein (16% of calories)

6% carbohydrates (61% of calories)

2 g fiber

25 mg sodium

Makes 6 servings

1. Toss the onion and bell peppers with the lime juice and set aside.

2. In a small bowl, mix the olive oil, orange juice, vinegar, garlic, scallion, thyme, and pepper and whisk to combine well.

3. In a bowl, toss the spinach and julienned radicchio, add the reserved onion and peppers, drizzle with vinaigrette, and toss well. Place the reserved radicchio leaves on chilled plates and spoon the salad on them. Garnish with mushrooms and thyme sprigs.

Taking the Ranch Home

We have choices in life every day. It seems simplistic, but in a profound way it can be very helpful to choose good thoughts, to *choose* to be positive. At the Ranch we have a gym—really more of a quiet meditation place—called *Milagro* (miracle) that looks out on Mt. Kuchumaa's serene eastern face. This is a wonderful spot to realize how often back home we waste time wishing we were somewhere else. When you don't have a Milagro to rest in, remember that what you focus on *now* can become powerful. What you hold in consciousness can become your reality. If you focus on negativity, you usher it into your daily affairs. Empower the positive. Give it strength.

Grilled Vegetable Salad with Red Pepper Vinaigrette

Once a month, late at night after work, I have a get-together with the kitchen and dining room crew. The sky is filled with stars above my home where thirty to forty of my amigas and amigos sit around listening to old-time Mexican music, relaxing after a busy day. Along with many dishes and grilling specialties, we always make tortillas. And when the barbecues are fired up, we often grill fresh vegetables from the garden, then squeeze lime over them in a sizzle of steam. Give this salad a try next time you spark up the coals.

1 roasted red bell pepper (pages 58–59)

2 tablespoons balsamic vinegar

2 tablespoons red wine vinegar

1 teaspoon extra-virgin olive oil

1 shallot, peeled and sliced

1 garlic clove, chopped

1 teaspoon chopped fresh rosemary

1/4 teaspoon white pepper

1 medium zucchini, trimmed and sliced 1/4-inch thick

1 medium yellow summer squash, trimmed and sliced 1/4-inch thick

1 red bell pepper, stemmed, seeded, and cut into triangles about 2 to 2 1/2 inches wide at bottoms

1 yellow bell pepper, stemmed, seeded, and cut into triangles about 2 to 2 1/2 inches wide at bottoms

1 green bell pepper, stemmed, seeded, and cut into triangles about 2 to 2 1/2 inches wide at bottoms

4 scallions, both green and white parts, trimmed

1 medium tomato, cut crosswise into 1/4-inch-thick slices

1 ear corn, quartered

Eight 6-inch corn tortillas

3 tablespoons grated queso fresco cheese (see Note)

Rainbow Salsa Cruda (page 33)

Per Serving (not including salsa):

223 calories

4 g total fat (14% of calories)

1 g saturated fat

2 mg cholesterol

9 g protein (14% of calories)

44 g carbohydrates (72% of calories)

9 g fiber

111 mg sodium

Makes 4 servings

NOTE: *Queso fresco cheese is Mexican cow's milk cheese that is available in Mexican and Latin markets, some specialty stores, and depending on the region of the country, supermarkets. Slightly salty and grainy, it is made from pressed fresh curds. Substitute ricotta or farmer cheese.*

1. To make the vinaigrette, place the roasted pepper, vinegars, olive oil, shallot, garlic, rosemary, and pepper in a blender or food processor and process until smooth. Cover and refrigerate.

2. Prepare a charcoal or gas grill or preheat the broiler.

3. Spray the zucchini, summer squash, peppers, scallion, tomato, and corn with vegetable oil. Place the vegetables on the grill (you may want to use a grill basket) and grill for 5 to 15 minutes, depending on the vegetables and their density, turning several times until lightly charred and tender. The squashes and tomato will cook more quickly than the pepper. The corn and scallions will take more time than the tomato, but less than the peppers. Remove the vegetables from the grill as they cook.

4. Wrap the tortillas in foil and warm them on the edge of the grill while the vegetables cook.

5. Lay 2 tortillas on each plate and top with lettuce. Spoon the grilled vegetables on the lettuce, and drizzle with the vinaigrette. Sprinkle the cheese on top, fold the tortillas in half, and serve with salsa on the side.

Corn and Cactus Salad

Nopales, which are the leaves of the prickly pear cactus, are becoming more popular. When peeled and cooked, they have a slightly tart flavor. In this salad the green of the cactus, yellow of the corn, red of the pepper, and purple of the onion make a colorful palette. This is a tasty luncheon salad, or you can serve it warm as a side dish at breakfast with Garden Eggs with Herbed Tofu (page 13). Fresh nopales and chiles de arbol can be found in the Latin or Mexican markets in the spring and summer months.

Per Serving:

74 calories

0 g total fat (5% of calories)

0 g saturated fat

0 mg cholesterol

4 g protein (16% of calories)

17 g carbohydrates (79% of calories)

4 g fiber

73 mg sodium

Makes 6 servings

2 nopales, peeled of all spines

Juice of 1 lime

1 ear of fresh corn

1/2 red onion, chopped

1/4 cup diced red bell pepper

1 scallion, sliced

1 garlic clove, mined

1 teaspoon chopped fresh oregano

1/4 cup drained capers

Pinch of toasted and crumbled chile de arbol (page 57)

1 cup sliced romaine lettuce

1/2 cup plain nonfat yogurt

6 sprigs fresh cilantro

2 limes, cut into wedges

1. Lightly spray a sauté pan with vegetable oil spray and toast the nopales for 3 to 5 minutes on each side, squeezing a little lime juice over each side. The cactus will exude a little juice. Lift from the pan and cut into thin strips about 1/2 inch long and 1/4 inch thick. Drain in a colander set over the sink.

2. Scrape the kernels from the ear of corn by holding the cob upright and cutting down with a sharp knife. In a dry sauté pan, toast the kernels over medium heat, tossing, for about 5 minutes or until lightly browned.

3. In a large bowl, combine the onion, pepper, scallion, garlic, oregano, capers, chiles, nopales, corn, and lettuce and toss well. Stir in the yogurt until well combined.

4. Scoop the salad onto plates and garnish with cilantro and lime wedges.

Ranch Barley Salad

A robust salad with a great combination of vegetables. Sometimes I add a roasted garlic clove and a chopped tomato to the simmering barley.

3/4 cup barley

3 cups Basic Vegetable Stock
(page 75) or water

2 tablespoons low-sodium soy sauce

1 teaspoon ground cumin

1 yellow bell pepper, stemmed,
seeded, and diced

1 red bell pepper, stemmed, seeded,
and diced

1 medium onion, diced

1 carrot, diced

1 celery rib, diced

1 pimiento, diced

4 to 6 tablespoons fresh lime juice

2 tablespoons teriyaki sauce

3 garlic cloves, minced

1 tablespoon chopped fresh oregano

1 tablespoon chopped fresh dill

1 teaspoon chopped lavender
flowers (optional)

Freshly ground black pepper

6 cups torn mixed greens

Per Serving:

132 calories

1 g total fat (4% of calories)

0 g saturated fat

0 mg cholesterol

4 g protein (13% of calories)

28 g carbohydrates (83% of calories)

1 g fiber

411 mg sodium

Makes 6 servings

1. In a large saucepan, combine barley, stock, soy sauce, and cumin and bring to a boil over high heat. Reduce the heat and simmer slowly, covered, about 45 minutes, or until the barley is tender and the liquid is absorbed. You may need to add more liquid as the barley cooks to keep it from drying out. Remove from the heat and set aside to cool.

2. In a large mixing bowl, toss together the bell peppers, onion, carrot, celery, pimiento, lime juice, teriyaki sauce, garlic, oregano, dill, and lavender flowers, if using. Season to taste with pepper. Fold in the cooled barley. Adjust the seasoning, cover, and refrigerate for at least 30 minutes before serving.

3. Divide the greens among 6 plates and top with the barley salad.

Lentil and Sun-Dried Tomato Salad

This refreshing Greek-style salad relies on lentils to boost the protein content without adding fat. I make it at home, too, because it is so healthy, easy, and tasty. Try it with warm pita bread.

DRESSING

1/4 cup red wine vinegar

1 teaspoon extra-virgin olive oil

1/2 cup dry-packed sun-dried tomatoes, chopped

1 tablespoon low-sodium soy sauce

1/4 teaspoon freshly ground black pepper

SALAD

1 teaspoon cardamom seeds

1 medium onion, chopped

1 celery rib, chopped

1 carrot, chopped

3 garlic cloves, minced

1/2 cup lentils, rinsed

6 cups Basic Vegetable Stock (page 75)

Salt and freshly ground black pepper

2 scallions, sliced

1 red bell pepper, stemmed, seeded, and sliced

1 medium zucchini, cubed

1/4 teaspoon chile powder

1 head romaine lettuce, coarsely chopped

1/4 cup crumbled feta cheese

3 limes, halved

Per Serving:

147 calories

3 g total fat (14% of calories)

1 g saturated fat

4 mg cholesterol

9 g protein (22% of calories)

26 g carbohydrates (64% of calories)

11 g fiber

354 mg sodium

Makes 6 servings

1. To make the dressing, mix the vinegar, olive oil, tomatoes, tamari, thyme and pepper. Set aside to allow the tomatoes to soften and the flavors to blend.

2. To prepare the salad, in a sauté pan, toast the cardamom seeds over medium heat for 2 or 3 minutes, until they begin to change color and smoke slightly. Remove from the heat and coarsely crush using a mortar and pestle, pepper grinder, rolling pin, or hammer. Set aside.

3. In a large saucepan or stockpot, heat the oil over medium heat and sauté the onion, celery, and carrot for about 5 minutes, until the vegetables begin to soften. Add the garlic, lentils, and stock and season with salt and pepper. Bring to a boil, reduce to a simmer, and cook for about 25 minutes or until the lentils are tender but still firm. Strain and transfer to a large bowl. Add the scallion, red pepper, and zucchini. Sprinkle the chile powder over the top and toss well. Cover and refrigerate for at least 1 hour until cold and the flavors blend.

4. Toss the lettuce with the dressing, feta, and some black pepper. Top the lettuce with the lentil salad. Sprinkle with the toasted cardamom seeds and garnish with the lime.

Black Bean Salad

Serve this hearty salad on its own as a luncheon side dish or as an entrée. Simply spoon some over mixed greens and garnish the dish with cucumbers, sliced onions, and quartered tomatoes.

BEANS

1 cup black beans, sorted and rinsed

1 medium onion, diced

2 garlic cloves

1 tablespoon chopped fresh oregano

4 cups Basic Vegetable Stock (page 75) or water, or more if needed

1 teaspoon low-sodium soy sauce

Freshly ground black pepper

SALAD

2 red or yellow bell peppers, stemmed, seeded, and diced

2 medium tomatoes, diced

1 red onion, diced

1 scallion, thinly sliced

2 garlic cloves

1/4 cup chopped fresh cilantro

1 tablespoon chopped fresh oregano

1/4 cup balsamic vinegar

2 to 3 tablespoons fresh lime juice

1 teaspoon olive oil

Low-sodium soy sauce

Freshly ground black pepper

Per Serving:

124 calories

1 g total fat (9% of calories)

0 g saturated fat

0 mg cholesterol

7 g protein (20% of calories)

24 g carbohydrates (71% of calories)

6 g fiber

141 mg sodium

Makes 8 servings

1. Put the beans in a large bowl and add about 10 cups of water. Soak for at least 8 hours or overnight, changing the waters a few times, if possible. Drain, discard the soaking liquid, and set the beans aside. (See pages 64–65 for tips on soaking beans.)

2. Lightly spray a large saucepan or stockpot with vegetable oil spray and sauté the onion, garlic, and oregano over medium heat for about 5 minutes until the onion is golden. Stir in the stock, beans, soy sauce and pepper to taste. Bring to a boil, reduce the heat, and simmer for about 1 1/2 hours, or until the beans are tender. Add more liquid as needed to keep the beans covered. Drain and set aside to cool.

3. In a mixing bowl, combine the bell pepper, tomato, red onion, scallion, garlic, cilantro, oregano, balsamic vinegar, lime juice, and olive oil. Adjust the flavor with soy sauce and pepper, or additional lime juice. Add the beans, toss, and chill for at least 1 hour.

Garbanzo Bean Salad

I use garbanzo beans (chickpeas) in soups, casseroles, and pureed in Hummus sin Tahini (page 66). Give the salad a Middle Eastern twist by sprinkling on a tablespoon of chopped fresh mint.

BEANS

1 cup garbanzo beans (chickpeas), sorted and rinsed

1 medium onion, diced

2 garlic cloves, chopped

1 tablespoon chopped fresh oregano, or 1 teaspoon dried

1 teaspoon low-sodium soy sauce

4 cups Basic Vegetable Stock (page 75) or water, or more if needed

Freshly ground black pepper

SALAD

1 medium onion, diced

2 red or yellow bell peppers, stemmed, seeded, and diced

1 medium tomato, diced

1 scallion, both white and green parts, thinly sliced

1 tablespoon minced garlic

1 tablespoon chopped fresh oregano

1/4 cup balsamic vinegar

1 tablespoon olive oil

Low-sodium soy sauce

Freshly ground black pepper

8 cups torn mixed greens

Per Serving:

88 calories

2 g total fat (25% of calories)

0 g saturated fat

0 mg cholesterol

3 g protein (14% of calories)

13 g carbohydrates (61% of calories)

1 g fiber

82 mg sodium

Makes 8 servings

1. To prepare the beans, put them in a large bowl and add about 10 cups of water. Soak for at least 8 hours or overnight, changing the water a few times, if possible. Drain and set aside.

2. Lightly spray a stockpot with vegetable oil spray and heat over medium heat. Sauté the onion, chopped garlic, and oregano for about 5 minutes, until the onion is golden. Add the beans, soy sauce, and stock. Bring to a boil over high heat, reduce the heat, and simmer for about 1 1/2 hours or until the beans are very soft. Keep the beans covered during cooking with stock or water, adding it as necessary. Drain but do not allow the beans to cool for more than a few minutes.

3. To prepare the salad, in a large bowl, combine the onion, bell pepper, tomato, scallion, garlic, oregano, vinegar, and olive oil. Add the hot beans and toss to mix thoroughly. Season with soy sauce and black pepper. Cover and refrigerate for 30 minutes.

4. Divide the greens among 8 plates and top with the bean mixture.

Couscous Salad

By itself, couscous is a bland but nutritious, coarse semolina flour made from durum wheat. For this salad, I add saffron for its exotic floral taste and golden yellow color. And I'll occasionally drop dried apricots, cran-berries, or currants into the hot water just before adding the couscous and setting the tightly covered pan aside to rest.

Per Serving:
155 calories
0 g total fat (2% of calories)
0 g saturated fat
0 mg cholesterol
6 g protein (14% of calories)
32 g carbohydrates (84% of calories)
1 g fiber
181 mg sodium
Makes 6 servings

1 1/4 cups Basic Vegetable Stock (page 75) or water

2 tablespoons low-sodium soy sauce

1 teaspoon saffron

1 cup uncooked couscous

1 medium zucchini, diced

1 yellow bell pepper, stemmed, seeded, and diced

1 medium onion, diced

1 carrot, diced

1 celery rib, diced

3 garlic cloves, minced

1 tablespoon chopped fresh basil

1 tablespoon chopped fresh oregano

4 to 6 tablespoons fresh lime juice

Freshly ground black pepper

6 cups torn mixed greens

1. In a small saucepan, heat the stock and soy sauce over medium heat. Crush the saffron and sprinkle over the stock while it heats. Bring to a boil and immediately remove from the heat.

2. Put the couscous in a bowl and pour the boiling stock over it. Stir gently, cover with a plate or plastic wrap, and set aside for 8 to 10 minutes, until the liquid is absorbed and the couscous is tender. Add more hot stock, if necessary, to hydrate the couscous. Stir the couscous to remove any lumps. Fluff with a fork and set aside to cool.

3. In a large bowl, toss the zucchini, pepper, onion, carrot, and celery together. Add the garlic, basil, oregano, and lime juice and toss again. Add the couscous and toss gently to mix. Cover and refrigerate for at least 30 minutes and up to 2 hours.

4. Divide the greens among 6 plates and top each with the couscous salad.

Kashi Salad

Not to be confused with kasha (crushed buckwheat groats), Kashi cereal is a blend of wholesome grains and seeds: red wheat, oats, winter wheat, brown rice, triticale, buckwheat, and sesame seeds. Kashi Breakfast Pilaf is sold in health food stores and some supermarkets. Do not confuse it with Kashi Puffed Grain Cereal.

1 cup Kashi Breakfast Pilaf, rinsed
1 3/4 cups Basic Vegetable Stock (page 75) or water
1/4 cup fresh lime juice
2 tablespoons low-sodium soy sauce
1 teaspoon ground cumin
1 yellow bell pepper, stemmed, seeded, and finely diced
1 carrot, finely diced
1 medium onion, finely diced

1 celery rib, finely diced
2 tablespoons finely diced pimiento
3 garlic cloves, minced
1 tablespoon chopped fresh dill
2 tablespoons teriyaki sauce
1/4 teaspoon freshly ground black pepper, or to taste
8 cups torn mixed baby greens
Orange-Ginger Vinaigrette (page 151)

Per Serving (not including vinaigrette):

34 calories
0 g total fat (5% of calories)
0 g saturated fat
0 mg cholesterol
1 g protein (16% of calories)
7 g carbohydrates (79% of calories)
0 g fiber
306 mg sodium

Makes 8 servings

1. Preheat the oven to 350°F.

2. In an 8 by-8-inch baking dish, combine the Kashi, stock, lime juice, soy sauce, and cumin, stir gently, cover with foil or a lid, and bake for about 1 hour and 20 minutes, or until the Kashi is tender and the liquid is absorbed. Remove the lid, fluff with a fork, and set aside to cool.

3. In a mixing bowl, combine the bell pepper, carrot, onion, celery, pimiento, garlic, dill, and teriyaki sauce and season with pepper. Add the cooled Kashi and toss to mix. Adjust the seasoning, cover, and refrigerate for at least 30 minutes before serving.

4. Divide the greens among 8 plates and top with the Kashi salad. Drizzle the vinaigrette over each salad and serve.

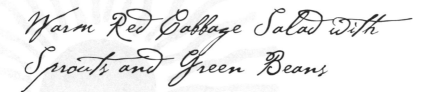

Warm Red Cabbage Salad with Sprouts and Green Beans

My wife Rosie makes this dish when cabbage is in season, which suits me to a tee since I come from a long line of cabbage eaters. My great grandma Fehlman's family, at one time, were the largest sauerkraut producers west of the Mississippi, but that's a story for another time.

1/2 teaspoon Asian sesame oil
1 red onion, chopped
3 garlic cloves, sliced
3 cups trimmed green beans
1 cup stemmed and sliced shiitake mushrooms
1 head red cabbage, shredded
4 cups mung bean sprouts
3 tablespoons low-sodium soy sauce
1 teaspoon chopped fresh cilantro

Place a sauté pan over medium-high heat and when the pan is very hot, add the oil and sauté the onion, garlic, beans, and mushrooms for about 2 minutes, just until the vegetables begin to soften. Add the cabbage and toss to mix. Add the sprouts and soy sauce and cook, tossing, for about 2 minutes longer, until well mixed and warm. Stir in the cilantro and serve.

Per Serving:
201 calories
2 g total fat (7% of calories)
0 g saturated fat
0 mg cholesterol
11 g protein (19% of calories)
44 g carbohydrates (74% of calories)
12 g fiber
648 mg sodium
Makes 4 servings

Taking the Ranch Home

Find a favorite quiet place in nature and revisit it . . . often. The Ranch is landscaped specifically to provide the walker with a daily discovery of new paths and hidden benches—yet no one ever seems to get "lost!" Even long-time visitors find a new way to walk to dinner that meanders past a boulder they've never seen before. Perhaps most beguiling, the Ranch's famous Yucatan hammocks hang like multi-colored cocoons in the shade of 400-year-old oaks, beckoning the afternoon reader or napper to enter their embrace.

Curried Rice Salad with Fruit

I learned how to bring out the herbal flavors of basmati rice from my colleague, Michel Stroot, executive chef at our sister spa, the Golden Door. Soaking the rice before cooking it plumps up the grains and using the soaking liquid make all the difference.

1 cup basmati rice

4 cups Basic Vegetable Stock (page 75) or water

1 teaspoon low-sodium soy sauce

1/2 teaspoon rice vinegar

1 teaspoon curry powder

1 tart apple, such as Granny Smith, peeled, cored, and cut into
   1/2-inch chunks

1/2 cup medium-diced pineapple, or one 8-ounce can pineapple
   chunks, drained

1 red bell pepper, stemmed, seeded, and cut into 2-inch julienne

2 celery ribs, diced

1/4 cup raisins

1/4 cup chopped walnuts

1 tablespoon chopped fresh cilantro

1/4 cup nonfat plain yogurt

1 head romaine lettuce, trimmed and chopped

1/2 cup chopped red leaf lettuce

1 cup julienned radicchio

1 cup chopped arugula

Spicy Chinese Celery Dressing (page 156) or Toasted Garlic
   Dressing (page 155)

**Per Serving
(not including
dressing):**

216 calories

4 total fat (15% of calories)

0 g saturated fat

0 mg cholesterol

7 g protein (12% of calories)

41 g carbohydrates (73% of
calories)

4 g fiber

64 mg sodium

Makes 6 servings

1. Put the rice in a sieve and rinse under cold running water, swishing it to separate the grains. Transfer to a bowl, add the stock, and set aside to soak for about 20 minutes. Drain, reserving 2 1/2 cups of the cooking liquid.

2. In a saucepan, combine the rice, the reserved stock, soy sauce, vinegar, and curry powder and bring to a boil over medium-high heat. Reduce the heat and simmer very slowly for 30 to 35 minutes, until the rice is tender and the liquid is absorbed. Fluff the rice with a fork and set aside to cool.

3. In a mixing bowl, toss the apple, pineapple, pepper, celery, raisins, walnuts, cilantro, and yogurt until the fruit and vegetables are well coated with yogurt. Add the rice and toss to mix well.

4. In another bowl, toss the romaine, red leaf lettuce, radicchio, and arugula. Divide among 6 plates and top with the rice salad. Drizzle each with a little dressing and serve.

How to Cut a Mango

Mangoes are among the most beautiful and luscious of all fruit—but they can be a mess to eat! Before Rigoberto Ramirez, my right hand in the Ranch kitchen, taught me how to cut one, I had mango juice dripping down my arm every time I attempted eating one.

Rigo explained that the secret to mango success is to cut the fruit next to its large flat seed, rather than trying to cut around the seed. Find the small hump on the lengthwise ridge running along the top of every mango. Set the oblong shaped mango on a cutting board with the ridge facing up, put your finger on the hump, and position a small sharp knife just slightly to the outside of the ridge. Cut straight down, so that you are slicing the fruit next to the seed. If you hit the seed, move the knife a little farther away from the ridge. Slice all the way through and set aside this first of three sections of the mango. Next, cut along the other side of the seed and set this seed-free section with the other one.

Hold the third section, the one with the seed, by the skin and make a slice through the skin, peeling it slowly and carefully back a few inches. The mango fruit surrounding the seed beneath that section of skin can be cut away at this point. Peel the skin back a little more, cutting away the fruit as you go. Finally, scoop or cut the fruit from the other two sections, holding them by the skin.

For a pretty garnish, using a small sharp knife, score the seed-free mango flesh in a cross-hatch or fan pattern. Holding it gently and pressing your fingers under the mango section against the skin, push up and out so that the fruit "pops up," still attached to the skin, and looks decorative and pretty. Anyone who has eaten breakfast or lunch at the Ranch will recognize this method of presenting mangoes.

Spa Tropical Fruit Salad with Toasted Quinoa

I love tropical fruit, and I had my first opportunity to taste what is now my favorite variety of papaya when I was working in Guaymas, Mexico. These big papaya from central or southern Mexico are sweet and almost floral in taste. Never—and I mean never—walk under one of these papaya trees because the fruit are like small Volkswagens barely hanging by little stems. I've cut up papayas shipped to the Ranch in Baja California that were as long as three footballs laid end to end. This salad is even more delicious when topped with a sprinkle of quinoa to give it a nutty crunch.

4 teaspoons quinoa

1/2 cup nonfat plain yogurt

1/4 teaspoon ground cinnamon

1 teaspoon grated orange zest

2 mangoes, halved and fanned
 (page 136)

3/4 cup peeled and sliced papaya

3/4 cup peeled and sliced honeydew
 melon

2 cups strawberries

3/4 cup peeled and sliced pineapple

4 mint leaves, for garnish

4 limes, halved

Per Serving:

195 calories

1 g fat (5% of calories)

0 g saturated fat

1 mg cholesterol

4 g protein (8% of calories)

49 g carbohydrates (87% of calories)

8 g fiber

33 mg sodium

Makes 4 servings

1. In a dry sauté pan, toast the quinoa over medium heat for 2 or 3 minutes, until lightly browned. Transfer to a plate to stop the cooking.

2. In a small bowl, combine the yogurt, cinnamon, and zest and stir to mix.

3. Set a mango fan on each chilled plate and arrange the sliced fruit around it. Spoon the yogurt in the center, then garnish with mint leaves, lime halves and a sprinkling of toasted quinoa.

Yogurt and Spiced Apple Salad

Here's a very popular salad that is often requested by returning guests, who can't wait to get back and have it for lunch. Jesus Tapia, one of our young cooks, usually prepares it, and around the kitchen we call this Tapia's Apple Salad.

1/4 cup nonfat plain yogurt
1/4 cup unfiltered, unsweetened apple juice
1 tablespoon raisins or currants
1 tablespoon sunflower seeds
1 teaspoon coconut flakes
1 teaspoon fresh lime juice
1/2 teaspoon vanilla extract
1/2 teaspoon ground cinnamon
4 Golden or Red Delicious apples

1. In a mixing bowl, combine the yogurt, apple juice, raisins, sunflower seeds, coconut, lime juice, vanilla, and cinnamon.

2. Core the apples and cut into thin wedges or bite-size pieces. Toss the apples in the yogurt mixture and refrigerate for at least 30 minutes before serving.

Per Serving:

84 calories

1 g total fat (14% of calories)

0 g saturated fat

0 mg cholesterol

1 g protein (5% of calories)

17 g carbohydrates (81% of calories)

1 g fiber

9 mg sodium

Makes 6 servings

Carrot-Ginger Salad with Pineapple

The union of pineapple and ginger with the sweetness of the carrots makes this salad especially refreshing.

3 carrots, grated

1/2 cup chopped pineapple

2 tablespoons raisins

1 garlic clove, minced

1/2 teaspoon minced fresh ginger

1/4 teaspoon Asian sesame oil

1/4 cup rice vinegar

1/4 teaspoon brown sugar

1/4 teaspoon hot red pepper flakes

1 head radicchio

1 head red leaf lettuce

1 head butter lettuce

1 tablespoon sesame seeds, toasted

Per Serving:

58 calories

1 g total fat (19% of calories)

0 g saturated fat

0 mg cholesterol

2 g protein (14% of calories)

11 g carbohydrates (67% of calories)

2 g fiber

20 mg sodium

Makes 6 servings

1. In a bowl, combine the carrot, pineapple, raisins, garlic, ginger, oil, vinegar, brown sugar, and red pepper flakes. Toss and refrigerate for 15 to 20 minutes so the flavors blend.

2. Separate 6 leaves from the radicchio and set aside. Tear the remaining lettuces, including radicchio, into pieces. Place in a bowl and toss. Place a radicchio leaf in the center of each plate and arrange the torn leaves on top. Scoop the carrot salad onto each plate and sprinkle with toasted sesame seeds.

Cucumber-Papaya Salad

In Mexican cooking it is very common to combine something sweet with a little chile fire. This salad gets its liveliness from a touch of Vietnamese chile sauce and some fresh ginger, banana, and cilantro.

Per Serving:
130 calories
2 g total fat (17% of calories)
0 g saturated fat
0 mg cholesterol
4 g protein (13% of calories)
23 g carbohydrates (70% of calories)
2 g fiber
76 mg sodium
Makes 6 servings

DRESSING

1/4 cup plus 2 tablespoons fresh lime juice

1/4 cup rice vinegar

2 tablespoons minced fresh ginger

2 scallions, both green and white parts, trimmed and thinly sliced on the bias

2 tablespoons chopped fresh cilantro

1/4 teaspoon Vietnamese-style chile sauce

Pinch of brown sugar

SALAD

1 head radicchio, leaves torn into bite-size pieces

1 pound spinach, stemmed and well washed

1 1/2 cups peeled, seeded, and sliced papaya (in slices about 1 inch long)

1 cucumber, peeled, halved, seeded, and thinly cut on the bias

1 banana, cut into 1/2-inch slices

1 cup diced pineapple

2 tablespoons sunflower or sesame seeds, toasted

1. To make the dressing, combine the ingredients in a small bowl, whisk well, cover, and refrigerate.

2. To assemble the salad, toss the radicchio and spinach together and set aside.

3. Put the papaya, cucumber, banana, and pineapple in a mixing bowl. Add the dressing and toss gently until combined.

4. Arrange the salad greens on chilled plates and spoon the fruit over them. Sprinkle with toasted seeds.

Roasted Red Potato Salad

When roasting the potatoes in the oven, let them reach a toasty brown color without burning (overdone potatoes will be bitter). Shake the sheet pan occasionally as they bake.

Per Serving:

156 calories

1 g total fat (5% of calories)

0 g saturated fat

0 mg cholesterol

6 g protein (15% of calories)

32 g carbohydrates (80% of calories)

3 g fiber

272 mg sodium

Makes 6 servings

2 tablespoons balsamic vinegar

2 tablespoons rice vinegar

2 garlic cloves, minced

1/2 teaspoon chopped fresh rosemary

Pinch of hot red pepper flakes

Pinch of freshly ground black pepper

1/2 teaspoon olive oil

4 large red potatoes (about 2 pounds), cut into 1/2-inch pieces

3 hard-cooked large egg whites, chopped

1/2 red onion, diced

1 celery rib, diced

1 medium tomato, diced

1 teaspoon minced fresh oregano

2 tablespoons coarse-grain Dijon mustard

2 tablespoons nonfat plain yogurt

1. Preheat the oven to 400°F. Lightly coat a baking sheet or large baking pan with vegetable oil.

2. In a large bowl, combine the vinegars, garlic, rosemary, pepper flakes, pepper, and oil and whisk to mix. Add the potatoes, toss, and then drain the excess marinade, saving 2 tablespoons. Spread the potatoes on the baking sheet and bake for about 45 minutes, until golden brown. It may be necessary to turn the potatoes as they bake to prevent burning.

3. In the bowl used to toss the potatoes, combine the egg whites, onion, celery, tomato, oregano, mustard, reserved marinade, and yogurt. Toss the browned, hot potatoes with the ingredients in the bowl. Serve warm or refrigerate for at least 30 minutes to allow the flavors to come together.

Summer Vegetable and Noodle Salad

Create your own version of this salad by adding or substituting your favorite vegetables—it need never be the same.

DRESSING

1 tablespoon rice vinegar

2 tablespoons balsamic vinegar

3 garlic cloves, minced

1 scallion, finely sliced

1 tablespoon chopped fresh basil

1 teaspoon chopped fresh cilantro

1/2 teaspoon freshly ground black pepper

SALAD

1/2 pound cellophane noodles

1 teaspoon Asian sesame oil

1 pound mixed salad greens, such as Bibb lettuce, arugula or watercress, chopped

1 head radicchio, torn into bite-size pieces

2 cups cherry tomatoes (about 12 tomatoes), left whole or halved if very large

3 small eggplant, quartered and sliced

1/4 pound shiitake mushrooms, stemmed and sliced

1 tablespoon rice vinegar

1 red bell pepper, stemmed, seeded, and sliced

1 yellow bell pepper, stemmed, seeded, and sliced

1 cucumber, cubed

1 cup broccoli florets, blanched

2 scallions, sliced on the bias

Per Serving:

274 calories

2 g total fat (6% of calories)

0 g saturated fat

0 mg cholesterol

11 g protein (15% of calories)

59 g carbohydrates (79% of calories)

10 g fiber

733 mg sodium

Makes 6 servings

1. To make the dressing, combine all the ingredients in a glass or ceramic bowl, add 2 tablespoons water, and whisk well. Set aside.

2. To prepare the salad, in a large bowl, soak the noodles in boiling water for 10 to 12 minutes, until softened. Drain and return to the bowl. Toss with the sesame oil and 1/4 cup of water. Set aside.

3. Toss the mixed greens, radicchio, and cherry tomatoes together and divide among 6 plates.

4. Place the eggplant and mushrooms in a medium sauté pan heated over medium-high heat. Toss to prevent burning, and sprinkle with vinegar; sauté for about 2 minutes, until the vegetables just begin to soften. Remove from the heat and add the bell peppers, cucumber, broccoli, and scallions. Add the noodles and toss gently to mix. Divide among the plates, spooning the vegetable-pasta mixture over the greens. Drizzle about 2 tablespoons of dressing over each salad and serve.

NOTE: *To blanch the broccoli florets, cook them in lightly salted boiling water for about 1 minute, until they turn bright green and are barely fork-tender. Drain, rinse with cold water to stop the cooking, and set aside.*

Warm Mexican Pasta Salad with Herbed Tofu

Tofu is quite bland and smooth, but marry it with some herbs in a pasta salad, and it adds enough low-fat, no-cholesterol protein to create a most satisfying lunch.

1/2 pound firm tofu, drained
  (pages 186–187)
1/2 pound fresh or dried fettuccine
1 teaspoon olive oil
1/2 medium onion, julienned
1/2 carrot, cut into 2-inch julienne
1 red bell pepper, stemmed, seeded,
  and cut into 2-inch julienne
1 medium zucchini, cut into 2-inch
  julienne
1/4 pound shiitake mushrooms,
  stemmed and sliced

4 garlic cloves, sliced
1 jalapeño pepper, stemmed and
  sliced
1 tablespoon chopped fresh oregano
1 tablespoon chopped fresh basil
1 medium tomato, chopped
1/2 cup Basic Vegetable Stock
  (page 75) or water
Freshly ground black pepper
2 tablespoons crumbled feta cheese
6 sprigs each fresh basil and oregano,
  for garnish

Per Serving:
225 calories
4 g total fat (14% of calories)
1 g saturated fat
2 mg cholesterol
11 g protein (18% of calories)
41 g carbohydrates (68% of calories)
5 g fiber
97 mg sodium
Makes 6 servings

1. Cut the tofu into 1/2-inch cubes and set aside.

2. Cook the pasta as directed until al dente, drain, and set aside.

3. In a large sauté pan, heat the oil over medium-high heat and sauté the onion, carrot, red pepper, zucchini, mushroom, and garlic for about 5 minutes, until the onion is golden. Add the tofu, jalapeño, oregano, basil, and tomato and cook for about 1 minute, tossing, until well mixed. Add the stock and pasta and cook, tossing, for 1 to 2 minutes, until heated through. Season with pepper, top with feta, and garnish with basil and oregano sprigs.

Taking the Ranch Home

Achieve balance in your fitness workout or lifestyle: Think of an exercise "triangle" composed of aerobics, strength, and flexibility. *Aerobics:* Work aerobically at least three times a week for an hour (including warm up and cool down time). Spend 20 minutes of that time working out within your target heart rate (this can be determined with the aid of an exercise professional). Even a half-hour of aerobic exercise has benefit. *Strength:* In 20 minutes, twice a week minimum, you can aid and maintain muscle mass. *Flexibility:* Do a little stretching each day, and have a good 20-minute or more stretch session at least twice a week.

This balanced "formula"—along with treatments such as massage, steam and whirlpool baths, and herbal wraps—is effective at staving off really uncomfortable soreness at Rancho La Puerta, even when guests launch into the week-long program after having spent months, or years, with little prior daily fitness activity.

Papaya-Lime Dressing

Most papaya lovers don't complicate the experience very much: they dig at the creamy fruit with a spoon, squeezing lime as they go. And that's great, but we like to let that same delicious taste envelope an entire fruit salad, or even a dessert.

1 cup peeled and chopped papaya (about half a papaya)
1 tablespoon fresh lime juice
1 tablespoon grated lime zest
1/4 teaspoon vanilla extract

In a blender or food processor, combine all the ingredients and process until smooth. Adjust the seasoning. Serve at once or refrigerate for up to 2 days. Whisk before serving.

Per 2 Tablespoons:

7 calories

0 g total fat (3% of calories)

0 g saturated fat

0 mg cholesterol

0 g protein (6% of calories)

2 g carbohydrates (91% of calories)

0 g fiber

1 mg sodium

Makes about 1 cup

NOTE: *Because Rancho La Puerta is located in Mexico, I rely on the outstanding local papayas, which tend to be sweeter than their Hawaiian cousins. Look for very ripe, soft papayas for the sweetest fruit.*

Blue Cheese–Pepper Dressing

A base of nonfat yogurt, flavored with a bit of feta and blue cheese and plenty of vinegar, makes this a good substitute for your favorite creamy dressing. You can also serve it as a low-fat dip for vegetables and crisp fruit.

2 shallots, minced

2 garlic cloves, minced

1 scallion, chopped

1 tablespoon chopped fresh oregano

1/4 cup red wine vinegar

1/4 cup balsamic vinegar

1/2 cup nonfat plain yogurt

2 tablespoons crumbled feta cheese

2 tablespoons crumbled blue cheese

1 tablespoon freshly ground black pepper

In a blender, combine all the ingredients with 1/4 cup water and process until smooth. Adjust the seasonings. Serve at once or refrigerate for up to 2 days. Whisk before serving.

Per 2 Tablespoons:

24 calories

1 g total fat (27% of calories)

1 g saturated fat

3 mg cholesterol

2 g protein (22% of calories)

4 g carbohydrates (52% of calories)

0 g fiber

46 mg sodium

Makes about 1 1/2 cups

Caesar Dressing

Tijuana, an amazingly international city in Baja California, which shares a border with San Diego, has been the source of many great recipes. None is more famous than the classic anchovy, raw egg, and olive oil Caesar dressing invented many years ago by Italian restaurant owner Caesar Cardini. In my version I leave out the egg and oil so the fat content is a scant 1/2 gram per serving. Serve it over romaine, of course.

2 cups low-fat buttermilk
6 anchovy fillets, drained
1 shallot, chopped
2 garlic cloves, minced
1 tablespoon chopped fresh oregano
1/4 cup red wine vinegar
2 tablespoons grated Parmesan
1/4 cup finely chopped parsley
Sea salt

Place all of the ingredients in a blender and blend 5 to 7 seconds until smooth.

Per 1 1/2 Tablespoons:

22 calories

1 g total fat (24% of calories)

0 g saturated fat

3 mg cholesterol

2 g protein (32% of calories)

2 g carbohydrates (44% of calories)

0 fiber

49 mg sodium

Makes about 2 1/2 cups

Herbed Yogurt Nonfat Dressing

Another variation on my basic yogurt recipes (see also Blue Cheese–Pepper Dressing, page 147, and Orange-Yogurt Dressing, page 150). Note how I hold back the scallions from the blending step; you don't want to lose a bit of crunch and color. Experiment with any of your favorite herbs, but remember to use only half the amount if they are dried.

2 shallots, minced
2 garlic cloves, minced
1 tablespoon chopped fresh oregano
1/4 teaspoon chopped fresh cilantro
1 teaspoon chopped fresh thyme
1/4 cup red wine vinegar
1/4 cup balsamic vinegar
1/2 cup nonfat plain yogurt
1 teaspoon freshly ground black pepper
1 scallion, finely chopped

In a blender or food processor, combine all the ingredients except the scallion with 1/4 cup water and process until smooth. Stir in the scallion and adjust the seasonings. Serve at once or cover and refrigerate for up to 2 days. Whisk before serving.

Per 2 Tablespoons:

15 calories
0 g total fat (4% of calories)
0 g saturated fat
0 mg cholesterol
1 g protein (22% of calories)
3 g carbohydrates (74% of calories)
0 g fiber
10 mg sodium

Makes about 1 1/4 cups

Orange-Yogurt Dressing

Refreshing with fruit salad or even spooned over fruit cobblers, lemon pudding or thinly sliced cake.

1 cup fresh orange juice
1 cup nonfat plain yogurt
1/2 banana
1/2 teaspoon vanilla extract
1/4 teaspoon ground cinnamon

In a blender or food processor, combine all the ingredients and process until smooth. Adjust the seasoning. Serve at once or refrigerate for up to 2 days. Whisk before serving.

**Per Serving
(3 Tablespoons):**

37 calories

0 g total fat (4% of calories)

0 g saturated fat

1 mg cholesterol

2 g protein (21% of calories)

7 g carbohydrates (75% of calories)

0 g fiber

22 mg sodium

Makes about 1 1/2 cups

Orange-Ginger Vinaigrette

A light dressing that goes well with sliced cucumbers, zucchini, peaches, pears, or apples—or any combination of these!

1/2 cup fresh orange juice

1/4 cup rice vinegar

2 teaspoons low-sodium soy sauce

1 teaspoon Asian sesame oil

2 garlic cloves, minced

1/2 teaspoon minced fresh ginger

1 teaspoon chopped fresh thyme or basil

1 scallion, thinly sliced

In a blender or food processor, combine all the ingredients and process until smooth. Adjust the seasoning. Serve at once or refrigerate for up to 2 days. Whisk before serving.

Per Serving (2 Tablespoons):

16 calories

1 g total fat (33% of calories)

0 g saturated fat

0 mg cholesterol

0 g protein (6% of calories)

2 g carbohydrates (61% of calories)

0 g fiber

86 mg sodium

Makes about 1 cup

NOTE: *Whip in a spoonful of Dijon mustard for a zippy change.*

Chinese Ginger Dressing

I use this light, refreshing dressing on everything from simple green salads to roasted or grilled vegetables. It also makes a great marinade.

2 teaspoons low-sodium soy sauce

2 garlic cloves, minced

1/2 teaspoon minced fresh ginger

1 cup rice vinegar

1 teaspoon brown sugar

1 teaspoon Asian sesame oil

2 scallions, sliced

1 teaspoon chopped fresh cilantro

1/2 teaspoon hot red pepper flakes

In a small bowl, combine all the ingredients and whisk to mix. Serve at once or cover and refrigerate for up to 2 days. Whisk before serving.

Per 2 Tablespoons:

11 calories

1 g fat (30% of calories)

0 g saturated fat

0 mg cholesterol

0 g protein (5% of calories)

2 g carbohydrates (65% of calories)

0 g fiber

56 mg sodium

Makes about 1 1/4 cups

Pineapple Vinaigrette with Ginger and Thyme

I especially like this Indonesian-style salad dressing over *Tres Estrellas Salad* (page 108), *Cucumber-Papaya Salad* (page 140), and *Carrot-Ginger Salad* (page 139). Sometimes I add a few pinches of hot red pepper flakes.

1/2 cup chopped fresh pineapple

1/2 cup unsweetened, unfiltered apple juice

3 tablespoons rice vinegar

1 teaspoon chopped fresh thyme

1/2 teaspoon minced fresh ginger

1/2 teaspoon minced shallot

1/2 teaspoon minced garlic

1/4 teaspoon brown sugar

Freshly ground black pepper

In a blender or food processor, combine all the ingredients and process until smooth. Adjust the seasonings. Serve at once or refrigerate for up to 2 days. Whisk before serving.

Per 3 Tablespoons:

16 calories

0 g total fat (4% of calories)

0 g saturated fat

0 mg cholesterol

0 g protein (3% of calories)

4 g carbohydrates (93% of calories)

0 g fiber

1 mg sodium

Makes about 1 1/2 cups

Sun-Dried Tomato-Basil Dressing

Who wouldn't make this dressing regularly if he or she had—as we do at the Ranch—nine varieties of basil and seven varieties of tomato to choose from? Our basil never sees the inside of a plastic bag; we put the sprigs in water like fresh flowers as soon as we pick them. I never toss out the basil stems; they're destined for vegetable stock. Try this dressing over the best sliced tomatoes you can find, or toss it on your next cold pasta salad.

2 ounces dry-packed sun-dried tomatoes
2 shallots, minced
2 garlic cloves, minced
1 scallion, chopped
2 tablespoons chopped fresh basil
1 teaspoon chopped fresh cilantro
1/2 cup red wine vinegar
1/4 cup balsamic vinegar
1/2 cup nonfat plain yogurt
1/4 cup low-fat buttermilk
Freshly ground black pepper

1. Combine the ingredients plus 1/4 cup water and let sit for about 5 minutes to soften the tomatoes.

2. Transfer to a blender or food processor and process until smooth. Adjust the seasonings. Serve at once or refrigerate for up to 2 days. Whisk before serving.

Per 3 Tablespoons:
31 calories
0 g total fat (6% of calories)
0 g saturated fat
0 mg cholesterol
2 g protein (21% of calories)
7 g carbohydrates (73% of calories)
1 g fiber
135 mg sodium
Makes about 2 cups

Toasted Garlic Dressing

Toasting garlic and ginger in a very hot pan with a tiny amount of sesame oil marries their flavors in a unique way. Don't overcook or burn the garlic; it will turn bitter. Let this dressing sit for about an hour or so before serving.

1 teaspoon olive oil
8 garlic cloves, minced
2 tablespoons minced fresh ginger
1/2 cup low-sodium soy sauce
1/2 cup teriyaki sauce
1/2 teaspoon Asian sesame oil
3 tablespoons rice vinegar
1 teaspoon arrowroot or cornstarch

1. In a sauté pan, heat the olive oil over medium-high heat and sauté the garlic and ginger for about 5 minutes, until the garlic and ginger are golden brown. Take care not to burn the garlic. Reduce the heat to low and add the soy sauce, teriyaki sauce, and sesame oil to the pan and cook for about 15 seconds, until fragrant.

2. While sauce is cooking, mix the vinegar and cornstarch in a small bowl and pour into the sauce. Simmer slowly for about 1 minute; do not boil. Serve warm over vegetables or rice, or cool and serve with a cold salad.

Per 1 1/2 Tablespoons:
25 calories
1 g total fat (20% of calories)
0 g saturated fat
0 mg cholesterol
2 g protein (27% of calories)
4 g carbohydrates (53% of calories)
0 g fiber
1,000 mg sodium
Makes about 1 1/4 cups

Spicy Chinese Celery Dressing

Here's "a little bit different" dressing that guests think is delicious. Try it on any salad, but I especially like it tossed with mung beans or on tender, young green beans known as haricots vert. Like many of my other dressings, you'll need to shake it in a cruet or whisk it just before drizzling over salad. Add it to pasta or rice dishes, but personally, I like it best on a simple cucumber salad.

1/2 cup diced celery
1 tablespoon minced fresh ginger
1/2 cup diced red onion
1/4 cup rice vinegar
1/2 tablespoon Asian sesame oil
2 tablespoons low-sodium soy sauce
2 garlic cloves, minced
2 tablespoons fresh lemon juice
1/2 teaspoon Asian chile paste
1/2 teaspoon celery seed, toasted

In a blender or food processor, combine all the ingredients and process until smooth. Adjust the seasonings. Serve at once or refrigerate for up to 2 days. Whisk before serving.

Per 1/4 Cup:
24 calories
1 g total fat (41% of calories)
0 mg cholesterol
1 g protein (9% of calories)
3 g carbohydrates (50% of calories)
1 g fiber
171 mg sodium
Makes about 1 cup

Vietnamese Salad Dressing

Zanne Stewart of Gourmet magazine brought me back to Southeast Asia with a recipe similar to the one here. Vietnamese fish sauce added to this dressing is a great way to lend a refreshing zip to any salad. Fish sauce may not be vegetarian, but this dressing is so good, I wanted to include it anyhow.

1 serrano chile, stemmed, seeded, and sliced
Juice of 2 limes
2 tablespoons brown sugar
2 garlic cloves, minced
1/4 cup Vietnamese fish sauce (nuoc nam; see Note)
1/4 cup shredded carrot
2 tablespoons diced red onion

In a blender or food processor, combine all the ingredients and process until smooth. Adjust the seasonings. Serve at once or refrigerate for up to 2 days. Whisk before serving.

Per 1 Tablespoon:

40 calories
1 g total fat (24% of calories)
0 g saturated fat
1 mg cholesterol
0 g protein (4% of calories)
8 g carbohydrates (72% of calories)
1 g fiber
5 mg sodium

Makes about 3/4 cup

NOTE: *Vietnamese fish sauce, or nuoc nam, is sold in Asian groceries.*

Main Courses

THE RANCH'S HIGH-CEILINGED DINING ROOM *is shared by 150 talkative, excited guests every evening. Those here for the first time mingle with happy returnees from all over the world, and the dinner tables are wonderful arenas of lively conversation.*

The recipes included here have all received a "thumbs up" from guests over the years. Can you really cook Mexican food that's low in fat? You betcha; we prove it every week with our delicious (and ever-popular!) chiles rellenos. Also our enchiladas and roasted tamales. My lasagne is also a surprise—so delicious that guests can't believe it's low in fat.

Enchiladas with Salsas Mexicanas

Classic variations on enchiladas usually involve corn tortillas taking a brief swim in hot oil. Then they're dunked in a sauce, filled, and rolled—delicious, but mucho caloric. In this version, the tortillas are heated in a dry pan. The only fat hiding inside these is a small amount of feta cheese, and its sharp, salty flavor goes a long way. Don't forget to spoon some salsa over these before serving.

1/2 medium onion, chopped
1 red bell pepper, stemmed, seeded, and sliced
1/2 medium potato, diced
6 ounces white mushrooms, sliced
2 garlic cloves, minced
2 tablespoons chopped fresh oregano
1/4 teaspoon hot red pepper flakes
1/2 cup crumbled feta cheese
6 corn tortillas
1/4 cup Roasted Salsa Colorado (page 48) plus more for garnish
2 heads romaine lettuce leaves, sliced 1/4-inch-thick
Rosie's Z-Wah Tomatillo Salsa (page 45)
6 sprigs fresh cilantro
6 radishes

Per Serving (not including salsas):
138 calories
3 g total fat (20% of calories)
2 g saturated fat
8 mg cholesterol
7 g protein (20% of calories)
22 g carbohydrates (60% of calories)
7 g fiber
224 mg sodium
Makes 6 servings

1. Preheat the oven to 350°F. Lightly coat with vegetable oil spray an ovenproof baking dish large enough to hold 6 rolled tortillas.

2. In a large sauté pan lightly sprayed with vegetable oil spray, sauté the onion and red pepper for about 5 minutes, until softened. Add the potato, mushroom, and garlic and cook for 5 to 7 minutes longer or until the potatoes soften. Remove from the heat and stir the oregano and red pepper flakes into the vegetables. If necessary, drain excess liquid in a strainer or colander. The mixture should be neither dry nor wet, but should be moist. Add the feta cheese and mix well.

3. Heat a dry medium sauté pan or frying pan over low heat and warm each tortilla. Cover the hot tortillas with a cloth napkin or tea towel or place them in a plastic bag so they don't dry out. Tortillas are easier to work with when they have been warmed.

4. Ladle 1/4 cup of the Salsa Colorado into a pie tin or onto a plate and coat each tortilla on both sides. Place 2 tablespoons of the vegetable mixture in the lower part of each tortilla and roll it up. Carefully place them seam side down in the baking dish and cover with a lid or aluminum foil. Bake on the center rack of the oven for about 20 minutes, until the filling is hot and bubbling.

5. Center the romaine lettuce slices on warmed dinner plates and place an enchilada on top. Ladle both the salsas over the enchiladas and garnish with sprigs of cilantro and the radishes.

Black Bean Tostadas

Instead of purchasing deep-fried corn tortillas that are often cooked in coconut oil, we bake our own for a low-calorie, low-fat shell with great flavor and crunchy texture. Dip each tortilla in water very quickly and then spray it with vegetable spray. Place the tortillas on a rack in a 400° F oven with another wire rack on top of them to keep them from curling. Bake for 12 to 15 minutes. Watch them carefully, so they don't burn.

BEANS

1/4 cup pinto beans, sorted and rinsed
1/4 cup black beans, sorted and rinsed
1/2 medium onion, diced
2 garlic cloves, minced
1 to 3 ancho chiles, halved and seeded (see Note)
1 chile de arbol or other dried chile, stemmed, seeded, and chopped
4 cups Basic Vegetable Stock (page 75) or water, or more if needed
Freshly ground black pepper
1 tablespoon chopped fresh oregano
6 tablespoons fresh lime juice
1 teaspoon sea salt (optional)

TOSTADAS

Six 10-inch tostada shells or flour tortillas (see Note)
1 head romaine lettuce, thinly sliced
1 bunch fresh cilantro, stems trimmed
3/4 cup Rainbow Salsa Cruda (page 33)
6 tablespoons Pea and Broccoli Guacamole Dip (page 67)

Per Serving:

141 calories

4 g total fat (22% of calories)

1 g saturated fat

2 mg cholesterol

7 g protein (18% of calories)

22 g carbohydrates (60% of calories)

6 g fiber

101 mg sodium

Makes 6 servings

1. To prepare the beans, put them in a large bowl and add about 10 cups of water. Soak for at least 8 hours or overnight, changing the water a few times, if possible. Drain and transfer to a large saucepan.

2. Add the onion, garlic, chiles, and stock and season with pepper. Bring to a boil over high heat. Reduce the heat and simmer, covered, for about 2 hours or until the beans are soft, with the texture of a baked potato. Be sure the beans are completely covered with water during cooking. (A good test for doneness is to pinch a bean between your thumb and forefinger to test the consistency.) Drain the beans and reserve the cooking liquid.

3. Transfer the beans to a food processor and puree. Use the cooking liquid, if necessary, to adjust the consistency. Add the oregano, lime juice, and salt, if using, and mix well.

4. To assemble the tostadas, spread about 2 tablespoons of the bean puree in a thin layer on each tostada. Top each with a generous pinch of shredded lettuce, 2 tablespoons of salsa, and 1 tablespoon of guacamole.

NOTE: *If you use flour tortillas instead of the store-bought tostada shells, brush the tortillas with lightly beaten egg white and bake them in a 350°F oven for about 15 minutes, until toasted. The baked tortilla adds 80 calories and 2 grams of fat to the recipe. We don't use flour tortillas for tostadas at the ranch because, when made in large quantities, the tortillas become soggy. On the other hand, you can also bake corn tortillas if you want to make low-fat tostadas. Preheat the oven to 425°F. Dip each corn tortilla in clean water, shaking off excess water, and lightly spray each with vegetable spray. Lay the tortillas on top of the oven rack in a single layer, not touching. Cover the tortillas with another rack or screen so the tortillas won't curl up as they bake. Bake for about 18 minutes, until golden. Take care they don't burn.*

Chile Cheese Pie

This dish is always a huge hit. Anaheim chiles are mild and sweet, making them the perfect introduction to chiles for anyone who can't stand much heat. Whole chiles are up to six inches long, and they are layered into the casserole like floppy leaves. For my own taste, I jazz it up with a pinch of red pepper flakes.

6 large egg whites

2 1/2 cups low-fat cottage cheese

2 tablespoons grated Parmesan cheese

1 tablespoon low-sodium soy sauce

1/2 teaspoon ground cumin

2 tablespoons chopped fresh oregano

4 garlic cloves, minced

Pinch of hot red pepper flakes (optional)

Freshly ground black pepper

12 Anaheim chiles, roasted and seeded but left whole (see Note)

1 medium onion, chopped

1 medium tomato, chopped

4 scallions, sliced

1 cup corn kernels

1 1/2 ounces Monterey jack cheese, shredded

Per Serving:

179 calories

3 g total fat (12% of calories)

1 g saturated fat

6 mg cholesterol

20 g protein (41% of calories)

23 g carbohydrates (47% of calories)

4 g fiber

255 mg sodium

Makes 8 servings

NOTE: *If you cannot find Anaheim chiles, substitute Ortega canned whole chiles. A 14-ounce can will be adequate.*

1. Preheat the oven to 350°F.

2. In a large bowl, mix the egg whites with the cottage cheese, Parmesan, soy sauce, cumin, oregano, garlic, red pepper flakes, and pepper and set aside.

3. Spray a 9- by 12-inch ovenproof dish or casserole with vegetable oil spray and lay half of the chiles in it. Sprinkle the onion, tomato, scallion, and corn evenly over the chiles and pour the egg mixture over the vegetables. Layer the remaining chiles to cover the pie completely and sprinkle with the shredded cheese.

4. Cover the dish with a lid or aluminum foil and bake in the center of the oven for about 1 hour, until hot and bubbling. Remove the lid or foil and bake 10 minutes longer to brown the top. Let rest for 10 minutes before serving.

Taking the Ranch Home

Balance! Phyllis Pilgrim, fitness director at Rancho La Puerta, stresses balance during her lectures, especially at orientation. But she's not talking about teetering on one foot atop a nearby boulder. Consider the triangle a useful symbol to aid your attain balance. It should be equilateral, whether the sides are small or large in terms of time. On one side, *exercise.* On another, the quality and amount of *food* you eat. On the third, the *rest* you give yourself. Notice that word *give*. Rest is a gift to the body! Rest is sleep, of course, but it also is the nurturing things you do for yourself—a massage, a facial, an afternoon spent with a good book and no distractions. One need not close the eyes to rest!

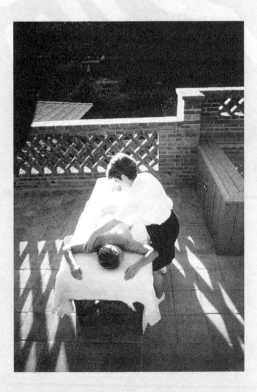

Chiles Rellenos

It's hard to imagine that chiles rellenos can be this good without frying them in fat. Our secret? We give them just a brief 3-minute sauté in a lightly oiled pan, then transfer them to an oven. The poblano is the chile of choice for chiles rellenos in Mexico, but at times poblanos can be a little too fiery. For more tender tongues, we use Anaheim chiles. They work well, but don't have the full flavor of the poblanos—you be the judge. Buen probecho. Serve these with Mexican Rice with Tomatoes (page 213), Mexican Black and Pinto Beans (page 210), and Roasted Salsa Colorado (page 48).

4 Anaheim or poblano chiles (about 3/4 pound)

1 ounce low-fat, low-sodium Monterey jack cheese, cut into 4 long strips

1 large egg white

1 large egg

1 garlic clove

1 teaspoon chopped fresh oregano

1/4 teaspoon salt

2 tablespoons whole wheat pastry flour

Per Serving:

84 calories

3 g total fat (30% of calories)

1 g saturated fat

58 mg cholesterol

6 g protein (28% of calories)

9 g carbohydrates (42% of calories)

0 g fiber

234 mg sodium

Makes 4 servings

1. Preheat the oven to 350°F.

2. Toast the chiles over an open flame until the skins are lightly charred. Transfer to a paper or plastic bag and let rest for 10 minutes. (Alternatively, roast the chiles in a baking pan in a preheated 400°F oven for 15 to 20 minutes, until the skin begins to pull away from the pepper.) Remove the skin to just below the stem of each chile. Make a 2-inch slit lengthwise in each chile and remove the seeds. Carefully insert one cheese strip in each chile.

3. Using an electric mixer set on medium-high speed, beat the egg white until doubled in volume. Beat in the whole egg, garlic, oregano, and salt until the mixture again doubles in volume or reaches soft peaks.

4. Sprinkle the flour on a plate and dredge the chiles with the flour to coat all sides.

5. Lightly spray a sauté pan with canola or olive oil spray and place over medium-high heat. Dip each chile into the egg batter and, working carefully, cook for about 1 1/2 minutes on each side. Lightly spray a baking pan with canola or olive oil spray. Transfer the chiles to the baking pan and bake for about 15 minutes, or until the cheese melts. Serve at once.

Roasted Tamale Pie

There are no corn husks in this tamale recipe—just the filling, which makes it easier to assemble. At the Ranch I use blue cornmeal, which fascinates diners who haven't encountered it before. Blue cornmeal—the color is entirely natural—is worth the search. In the Southwest, it's a staple right next to yellow and white cornmeal on grocery store shelves. But elsewhere you'll have to hit the gourmet stores to find it. Native Americans say that the blue color gives the diner long life and strength. And nutritionists agree: blue corn is 20 percent higher in protein, and has more zinc and iron than white or yellow cornmeal.

Mexican Marinade (page 171)
1 russet potato, thinly sliced
1/2 teaspoon olive oil
1 medium onion, chopped
4 garlic cloves, minced
1 medium zucchini, chopped
1 carrot, chopped
1/2 pound white mushrooms, sliced
2 tablespoons chopped fresh oregano
2 cups nonfat plain yogurt
6 large egg whites
1/2 teaspoon ground cumin
2 cups fresh corn kernels
1/4 cup stone-ground blue cornmeal
1 teaspoon freshly ground black pepper
2 ounces part-skim mozzarella cheese
1/2 cup grated Parmesan cheese
Shiitake-Tomatillo Sauce (page 55, optional)
6 tablespoons chopped fresh cilantro

Per Serving:
247 calories
6 g total fat (21% of calories)
3 g saturated fat
14 mg cholesterol
17 g protein (27% of calories)
34 g carbohydrates (52% of calories)
4 g fiber
373 mg sodium
Makes 8 servings

1. Preheat the oven to 375°F. Lightly spray a shallow 2- to 2 1/2-quart casserole with vegetable oil spray.

2. In a medium glass bowl, pour the marinade over the potato and set aside.

3. In a large sauté pan, heat the oil over medium-high heat and sauté the onion for about 3 minutes, until golden. Add the garlic, zucchini, and carrot and cook for 3 or 4 minutes, stirring until the vegetables begin to soften. Add the mushroom and oregano and cook for 2 minutes longer, until the mushrooms begin to exude their juices. Set aside.

4. In a blender, combine the yogurt, egg whites, cumin, corn, and corn-meal and process until smooth and pour over the vegetables. Add the pepper and cheeses and mix well.

5. Remove the potato from the marinade and layer the slices in the casserole. Spoon the vegetable-yogurt mixture over the potato slices and smooth over the top. Cover with a lid or foil and bake for 55 to 60 minutes, until hot and bubbling. Uncover the casserole and bake for a few minutes longer, until lightly browned. Let rest for about 10 minutes before serving with salsa and garnished with cilantro.

Taking the Ranch Home

It's one thing to eat healthfully three or more times a day when the Ranch is doing all the cooking. And we're also doing the grocery shopping and clean up. But what about at home, when the realities of an empty refrigerator and a lack of time after a long day have worn you down?

Two ideas that have worked for guests (they return and tell us so) are:

- When you do cook, make enough for more than one meal. Plan-overs, not leftovers, mean cooking more when you have the time, so you can eat well all the time.

- Some guests collaborate on healthful cooking by combining their efforts with friends, neighbors, or relatives—simpatico friends who share an interest in eating healthier food. They take turns cooking dinner on weeknights, effectively cutting the number of days each of them must cook by at least half. They say this method has returned a good measure of fun, satisfaction, and variety to their cooking.

Mexican Marinade

This is a great marinade and flavor enhancer for tofu and for any vegetables that will be roasted or baked.

1/4 cup red wine vinegar

1/4 cup white wine vinegar

Juice of 2 limes

1 teaspoon olive oil

3 garlic cloves, minced

1 teaspoon chopped fresh cilantro

1/4 teaspoon minced serrano peppers

1/4 teaspoon freshly ground black pepper

In a glass or ceramic bowl, combine all ingredients and mix well. Use immediately or cover and refrigerate for up to 1 month.

Per 1 1/2 Tablespoons:

15 calories

1 g total fat (28% of calories)

0 g saturated fat

0 mg cholesterol

0 g protein (4% of calories)

3 g carbohydrates (68% of calories)

1 g fiber

1 mg sodium

Makes about 3/4 cup

Corn and Feta Soufflé

Golden, ballooning soufflés are any professional or home chef's triumph. Here is a low-fat version that can stand alone as a main course. Serve it with Rosie's Z-wah Tomatillo Sauce (page 45) or Roasted Salsa Colorado (page 48).

1/2 teaspoon olive oil

1 shallot, minced

1 red bell pepper, stemmed, seeded, and diced

1 garlic clove, minced

2 tablespoons chopped fresh oregano

2 tablespoons chopped fresh basil

1/2 teaspoon freshly ground black pepper, or to taste

3 cups fresh kernels (from 3 or 4 ears corn)

1 medium all-purpose potato, peeled and minced

1 large egg yolk, lightly beaten

1 tablespoon unbleached all-purpose flour

3/4 cup low-fat cottage cheese

1 1/2 tablespoons crumbled feta cheese

2 tablespoons grated low-fat mozzarella cheese

6 large egg whites, at room temperature

Pinch of salt

8 sprigs fresh cilantro

Per Serving:

217 calories

5 g total fat (18% of calories)

2 g saturated fat

44 mg cholesterol

16 g protein (27% of calories)

32 g carbohydrates (55% of calories)

4 g fiber

460 mg sodium

Makes 6 servings

1. Preheat the oven to 375°F. Lightly butter a 2-quart soufflé dish.

2. To prepare the soufflé, heat the olive oil in a small sauté pan over medium heat and sauté the shallot for about 3 minutes, or until softened. Add the red pepper, garlic, oregano, basil, and black pepper and sauté for about 5 minutes longer, until the pepper softens. Transfer to a food processor, add the corn kernels, and process for about 30 seconds, just until chunky, not smooth. Scrape the mixture into a bowl, add the potato, stir to mix, and set aside.

3. In the bowl of an electric mixer set on medium speed, whisk the egg yolk until thick and lemon-colored (or use a whisk to beat the egg yolk). Add the flour and beat for about 1 minute to incorporate. Add the cottage cheese, feta, and mozzarella and stir to mix. Add about a quarter of the sautéed vegetables and stir to mix. Add the rest of the sautéed vegetables and stir again.

4. In a clean, dry bowl of an electric mixer, beat the egg whites at medium speed until frothy. Add the salt and increase the speed to medium-high and beat until stiff peaks form.

5. Fold about a third of the egg whites into the vegetable-cheese mixture. Gently fold in the remaining whites. Do not overmix or the egg whites will deflate. Immediately scrape the mixture into the soufflé dish. Set the dish in a roasting pan and pour enough hot water into the pan to come about 2 inches up the side of the dish. Smooth the top of the soufflé and bake on the center rack of the oven for 45 to 55 minutes, until raised and golden. Do not open the oven during baking or it may fall.

6. As soon as the soufflé is well risen, spoon it onto serving plates and garnish with sprigs of cilantro.

NOTE: *For the best results when beating egg whites, use room-temperature egg whites and a clean, dry bowl and clean, dry beaters. Beat the whites until stiff but not dry. Have all other ingredients mixed and ready to be folded with the beaten egg whites. In other words, don't "park" the beaten egg whites; gravity will work against them and their natural water content will settle to the bottom of the bowl.*

Classic Spa Lasagna

Without a doubt, this guilt-free recipe is the most requested one at the Ranch. I lower the fat and calories dramatically by featuring egg whites, nonfat cottage cheese, and tofu as the main filling ingredients, along with relatively small amounts of Parmesan and mozzarella cheeses. The absolutely fresh flavors of just-picked vegetables and rich plum tomato basil sauce meld together until you can almost taste the sunshine coming over Mt. Kuchumaa.

FILLING

1/2 cup egg whites

3/4 cup nonfat cottage cheese

1/4 cup grated mozzarella cheese

7 tablespoons grated Parmesan cheese

1/4 pound firm tofu, drained and crumbled

3 tablespoons minced garlic

2 tablespoons chopped fresh basil

1/4 teaspoon hot red pepper flakes

1/4 teaspoon freshly ground black pepper

VEGETABLES

1 teaspoon olive oil

1 red onion, chopped

1 red bell pepper, stemmed, seeded, and chopped

4 cups sliced white mushrooms

1/2 carrot, sliced

1 medium zucchini, chopped

2 tablespoons minced garlic

1/4 teaspoon freshly ground black pepper

2 tablespoons chopped fresh basil

4 cups Tomato-Basil Sauce (page 50)

1/2 pound (about 10 noodles) lasagna noodles, cooked and drained

Grated Parmesan cheese, for garnish

Per Serving:

272 calories

6 g total fat (19% of calories)

2 g saturated fat

11 mg cholesterol

16 g protein (24% of calories)

40 g carbohydrates (57% of calories)

3 g fiber

253 mg sodium

Makes 6 servings

1. Preheat the oven to 350°F.

2. To prepare the filling, in a large bowl, combine the egg whites, cheeses, tofu, garlic, basil, red pepper flakes, and black pepper. Mix gently, cover, and refrigerate.

3. To prepare the vegetables, in a large sauté pan over medium-high heat, heat the oil and cook the onion and pepper for 5 or 6 minutes, until softened. Fold in the mushrooms and sauté for about 5 minutes longer, until the mushrooms exude their juices. Add the carrot, zucchini, garlic, pepper, and basil and cook for 2 or 3 minutes, until heated through. Mix well and set aside.

4. In a 10 by 6 by 3-inch ovenproof dish or casserole lightly sprayed with vegetable or olive oil spray, spread about 1/3 cup of sauce. Layer in half the noodles, covering the entire bottom of the dish. Spread the cheese-egg filling evenly over the top of the noodles and then cover the filling with the cooled vegetables, slightly pressing to compress. Top with the remaining noodles. Spoon more sauce over the noodles and spread evenly. Cover with foil and bake in the center of the oven for about 1 1/2 hours, until the sauce is bubbling.

5. Let rest for 15 to 20 minutes. Cut equal portions and serve with the remaining warmed Tomato-Basil Sauce and the Parmesan cheese for sprinkling.

Pasta with Shiitake Mushrooms and Moroccan Lemons

Since Zanne Stewart, the food editor of Gourmet, *gave me a wonderful recipe for Moroccan lemons, I've slipped them into myriad dishes. I love pasta tossed with shiitake mushrooms and garlic, and when I add Moroccan lemons, there is an exquisite, buttery olive-lemon flavor without the fat.*

1/2 pound dried fettuccine or other pasta

1 tablespoon extra-virgin olive oil

3 garlic cloves, sliced

1/4 cup Basic Vegetable Stock (page 75) or water

2 cups stemmed and sliced shiitake mushrooms (about 4 ounces)

8 Moroccan Lemon wedges, minced (page 61)

3 tablespoons chopped fresh basil

Freshly ground black pepper

2 tablespoons grated Parmesan cheese (optional)

6 sprigs fresh basil

6 Moroccan Lemon wedges (page 61), for garnish

Per Serving:

199 calories

3 g total fat (15% of calories)

1 g saturated fat

28 mg cholesterol

6 g protein (13% of calories)

36 g carbohydrates (72% of calories)

2 g fiber

111 mg sodium

Makes 6 servings

1. In a pot filled with boiling water, cook the pasta until al dente, about 10 minutes. Drain and set aside.

2. In a large sauté pan, heat the oil over medium heat and sauté the garlic for about 2 minutes, until golden. (Take care not to burn the garlic.) Splash a little stock into the pan, then add the mushrooms, minced lemon, and basil and sauté for about 1 minute, until heated through. Add the remaining stock and cook for 30 seconds. Stir in the pasta, season to taste with pepper, and toss to mix.

3. Spoon onto warmed plates and dust with Parmesan cheese, if desired. Garnish with a sprig of basil and a wedge of Moroccan lemon.

Chile Pasta with Arugula and Coriander Seeds

Toasted chiles and coriander seeds add a smoky, spicy flavor that combines with the nutty taste of arugula to make this dish very special.

1 chile de arbol or other dried hot chile
2 tablespoons coriander seeds
1 pound fresh or dried fettuccine or linguine
2 teaspoons olive oil
3 garlic cloves, thinly sliced
6 cups chopped arugula leaves
1/4 cup grated Parmesan cheese

1. In a large, dry sauté pan, toast the chile over medium heat for 3 to 5 minutes, tossing, until lightly browned. Cool and then chop into small pieces.

2. Put the coriander seeds in the pan and cook, stirring, for 2 to 3 minutes, until browned and beginning to smoke. Cool and then crush in a mortar with a pestle, or with a rolling pin.

3. Cook the pasta in boiling water until al dente. Drain and cover to keep warm.

4. Add the oil to the hot pan and cook the chopped chile, coriander seeds, garlic, and arugula over medium heat for 1 to 2 minutes, until fragrant. Add the pasta and cheese and toss for about a minute, until heated through and mixed.

Per Serving:
269 calories
5 g total fat (17% of calories)
1 g saturated fat
59 mg cholesterol
12 g protein (17% of calories)
45 g carbohydrates (66% of calories)
0 g fiber
134 mg sodium

Makes 6 servings

NOTE: *When chopping chiles, never touch your eyes or mouth with your hands; after working with chiles, wash your hands in warm soapy water to prevent a burning sensation or other reaction.*

Pasta with Porcini and Sun-Dried Tomatoes

Mushrooms are one of my passions. I love them all, but porcini, cèpes, and morels are special because of their woodsy, earthy flavors. True, they tend to be expensive, but a few go a long way and are well worth the cost. I soak dried mushrooms in water to remove the grit and then I often cover them with brandy to infuse them with another layer of flavor.

Per Serving:

311 calories

3 g total fat (9% of calories)

1 g saturated fat

4 mg cholesterol

13 g protein (17% of calories)

59 g carbohydrates (74% of calories)

5 g fiber

210 mg sodium

Makes 6 servings

1 pound fresh or dried fettuccine

4 ounces dried porcini mushrooms

About 1/2 cup brandy

1 teaspoon olive oil

1/2 red onion, sliced

3 garlic cloves, minced

1/2 cup dry-packed sun-dried tomatoes

3 tablespoons chopped fresh basil

Pinch of freshly ground nutmeg

1/4 cup grated Parmesan cheese

Freshly ground black pepper

Fresh basil leaves, for garnish

1. Cook the pasta as directed until al dente, drain, and set aside.

2. In a small bowl, combine the mushrooms and enough brandy to cover. Set aside to soak for at least 20 minutes to plump the mushrooms. Drain and reserve the mushrooms and brandy.

3. In a large sauté pan, heat the oil over medium heat and cook the onion for 3 to 5 minutes, until golden. Add the garlic, drained mushrooms, and the brandy, if desired, and cook for about 2 minutes, until the mushrooms start to soften. Add the tomato, basil, and nutmeg and cook for about 1 minute, stirring, or until heated through.

4. Add the pasta and toss well. Serve sprinkled with Parmesan cheese and a generous sprinkle of pepper. Garnish with basil leaves.

Butternut Squash with Mushrooms

The fall-winter garden at Tres Estrellas is far from unproductive. Despite the sun's lower path across the south end of the valley, the rows are still bathed in warm light most of the day. Vine crops produce an amazing bounty, and golden butternut squash is one of my favorites to use in this hearty casserole. Sometimes I add a tablespoon of curry powder. The color combination is like melting gold into even more gold.

1/2 teaspoon olive oil

1 medium onion, diced

1 carrot, diced

1 celery rib, trimmed and diced

2 pounds butternut squash, peeled, seeded, and diced

1 medium all-purpose potato, diced

6 ounces white mushrooms, stemmed and quartered

1/2 cup cauliflower florets

4 garlic cloves, minced

6 large egg whites

1 cup low-fat cottage cheese

1/4 cup crumbled feta cheese

1/4 cup grated Parmesan cheese

2 tablespoons chopped fresh basil

1 tablespoon chopped fresh oregano

Freshly ground black pepper

Per Serving:

163 calories

3 g total fat (14% of calories)

2 g saturated fat

7 mg cholesterol

14 g protein (33% of calories)

23 g carbohydrates (53% of calories)

2 g fiber

285 mg sodium

Makes 6 servings

1. In a large sauté pan or skillet, heat the oil over medium heat and sauté the onion, carrot, and celery for about 5 minutes, until the onion is golden. Add the squash, potato, mushrooms, cauliflower, and garlic and sauté for about 5 minutes longer, until heated through. Set aside to cool slightly.

2. Preheat the oven to 350°F. Lightly spray a 9 by 12-inch baking dish with vegetable oil spray.

3. In a large mixing bowl, whisk the egg whites until frothy. Whisk in the cheeses, basil, oregano, and pepper to taste. Fold in the vegetables.

4. Spoon the mixture into the pan and press lightly to remove any air bubbles. Cover with foil or a lid and bake for about 1 hour, until hot and bubbling. Let stand for 10 minutes before serving.

Vegetarian Chili

Originally from Indonesia, tempeh has a third more protein than soybeans and adds a meaty texture that many of us expect from a hearty chili. I serve this over Mexican Rice with Tomatoes (page 213), and it's especially popular on those rare winter nights when the Ranch gets a frost.

Per Serving:

224 calories

3 g total fat (10% of calories)

0 g saturated fat

0 mg cholesterol

14 g protein (23% of calories)

40 g carbohydrates (67% of calories)

10 g fiber

264 mg sodium

Makes 8 servings

BEANS

1 cup black beans, sorted and rinsed

1/2 cup pinto beans, sorted and rinsed

1 medium onion, chopped

1 carrot, chopped

2 garlic cloves, chopped

1 tablespoon chopped fresh oregano

2 quarts Basic Vegetable Stock (page 75) or water

Salt and freshly ground black pepper

CHILE SAUCE

2 cups Basic Vegetable Stock (page 75) or water

3 ancho chiles, toasted (pages 56–57)

3 California chiles, toasted (pages 56–57)

1 medium onion, chopped

4 garlic cloves, chopped

2 medium tomatoes, chopped

2 bay leaves

1 tablespoon chopped fresh oregano

1 tablespoon chopped fresh cilantro

VEGETABLES

1/2 teaspoon olive oil

1 medium onion, diced

1 carrot, diced

1 celery rib, diced

1 medium zucchini, diced

1 green bell pepper, stemmed, seeded, and sliced

1/2 pound white mushrooms, quartered

4 garlic cloves, minced

1/4 pound tempeh, crumbled (see Note)

4 tablespoons chopped fresh cilantro, for garnish

4 tablespoons chopped onion, for garnish

1. To prepare the beans, put them in a large bowl and add about 10 cups of water. Soak for at least 8 hours or overnight, changing the water a few times, if possible. Drain and set aside. (See pages 64–65 for tips on soaking beans.)

2. Lightly spray a stockpot with vegetable oil spray and sauté the onion and carrot over medium-high heat for about 5 minutes, until the onion is golden. Add the beans, garlic, oregano, and stock and season to taste with salt and pepper. Bring to a boil over high heat. Reduce the heat and simmer, covered, for about 1 1/2 hours or until the beans are soft, with the texture of a baked potato. Be sure the beans are completely covered with water during cooking. (A good test for doneness is to pinch a bean between your thumb and forefinger to test the consistency.) Drain the beans and reserve 2 cups of the cooking liquid. Return the beans to the stockpot.

3. To make the chile sauce, heat the stock in a saucepan over medium heat. Add the chiles, onion, garlic, tomatoes, and bay leaves and bring to a simmer. Cook, simmering, for about 15 minutes and then set aside to cool.

4. Remove the bay leaves and transfer the mixture to a blender or food processor. Add the oregano and cilantro and process until pureed. Set aside.

5. To prepare the vegetables, heat the olive oil in a sauté pan over medium-high heat and sauté the onion, carrot, and celery for about 5 minutes, until the onion is golden. Reduce the heat, then add the zucchini, green pepper, mushroom, garlic, and tempeh and stir to mix. Cook for about 5 minutes longer, until the vegetables are warm but still firm. Do not overcook.

6. To assemble the chili, add the chile sauce and vegetables to the stockpot with the beans and stir gently. Bring to a simmer over low heat and cook, stirring occasionally, for about 10 minutes. Add as much of the reserved cooking liquid as needed to maintain a thick consistency; the chili should not be dry or soupy. Season to taste with salt and pepper.

7. Spoon into 8 bowls and garnish each serving with chopped cilantro and onion.

NOTE: *Tempeh is a soy product made by culturing soybeans with a beneficial bacteria and pressing the beans into thin cakes. It shares the health benefits of tofu, but is higher in fiber. The culturing gives the tempeh a pleasingly yeasty flavor that many nonvegetarians like, often preferring it to tofu. It is always served cooked. Tempeh cakes are sold in health food stores.*

Vegetable Quesadillas with Tofu

In Mexico, the eat-out-of-hand foods like tacos, burritos, and quesadillas are much smaller than the stuffed fast-food giants found north of the border. A quesadilla, instead of being a huge, fat-laden flour tortilla dripping with melted cheese, can be a delightful, small half-moon with just a touch of filling. Keep turning them in the pan until the tortilla is very hot and the filling melts. For a smoky flavor, substitute toasted chiles de arbol for the jalapeño.

2 tablespoons crumbled feta cheese

2 tablespoons grated low-fat mozzarella cheese

2 ounces firm tofu, crumbled (see Note)

1/2 teaspoon olive oil

1/2 red onion, diced

1/2 jalapeño pepper, chopped

1 garlic clove, minced

1/2 medium tomato, chopped

1 scallion, sliced

1 medium zucchini, chopped

1/2 cup fresh corn kernels

1 tablespoon chopped fresh cilantro

Freshly ground black pepper

6 corn tortillas

Per Serving:

121 calories

3 g total fat (20% of calories)

1 g saturated fat

4 mg cholesterol

5 g protein (16% of calories)

21 g carbohydrates (64% of calories)

3 g fiber

81 mg sodium

Makes 6 servings

NOTE: *To drain the tofu, put it in a colander set over a bowl and refrigerate for at least 20 minutes. Discard the drained water.*

1. In a bowl, mix the cheeses and tofu, cover, and refrigerate until ready to use.

2. In a large sauté pan, heat the oil over medium heat and sauté the onion, jalapeño, garlic, tomato, scallion, zucchini, and corn for about 2 minutes, until the vegetables start of soften. Add the cilantro and pepper to taste. Set aside in a colander set over a bowl and drain.

3. Place the tortillas in a hot, dry sauté pan over medium heat or on a hot grill. Warm until pliable, and then spoon 2 tablespoons of the vegetables and 2 tablespoons of the cheese-tofu mixture onto each. Fold the tortillas in half and toast for about 2 minutes on each side, or until the quesadillas are lightly browned. Serve hot.

Twice-Baked Saffron Potatoes

When I serve twice-baked potatoes at the Ranch, guest always offer me high fives. If I don't mention the tofu, nobody guesses! The saffron, though expensive, goes a long way to add golden color and delicate flavor. Serve this for lunch or dinner—or even for brunch.

4 russet potatoes
1/2 teaspoon olive oil
1/2 red onion, diced
1 celery rib, diced
1 small carrot, diced
1/2 cup diced broccoli florets
1 tablespoon minced garlic
1 1/2 teaspoons chopped fresh
  oregano
1/4 teaspoon crumbled saffron

2 ounces firm tofu, drained and
  crumbled (pages 186–187)
1/4 cup nonfat cottage cheese
1/4 cup grated Parmesan cheese
1/4 cup crumbled feta cheese
6 large egg whites
2 tablespoons minced flat-leaf
  parsley
Freshly ground black pepper

Per Serving:

224 calories

5 g total fat (20% of calories)

2 g saturated fat

10 mg cholesterol

17 g protein (29% of calories)

29 g carbohydrates (51% of calories)

4 g fiber

294 mg sodium

Makes 4 servings

1. Preheat the oven to 375°F.

2. Bake the potatoes for 40 to 45 minutes, until thoroughly cooked. Set aside to cool. Do not turn off the oven.

3. In a medium sauté pan, heat the oil over medium heat and sauté the onion, celery, and carrot for 3 to 4 minutes, until the onion softens. Add the broccoli, garlic, oregano, and saffron and cook for 1 minute longer, just to give the flavors time to meld.

4. Transfer to a large bowl and add the tofu, cottage cheese, Parmesan cheese, feta cheese, egg whites, and parsley and season to taste with pepper. Mix well.

5. When the potatoes are cool enough to handle, slice the tops lengthwise and scoop out the soft white centers without breaking the skin. Set the potato shells aside. Mix the potato pulp with the vegetable-tofu mixture, mashing the potato. Spoon equal portions into the shells.

6. Place the potatoes in an ovenproof dish and bake for about 20 minutes, or until the tops are lightly golden. Serve hot.

Roasted Tofu with Mango and Red Pepper Stir-Fry

Fruit? In a stir-fry? Mango, which comes into season in mid-February and is available throughout the summer, is a versatile component in this very popular main course at the Ranch. I find that tofu has more of a desirable al dente texture when it's first frozen, then thawed just before it's used. Before cutting, press out extra moisture, then stir-fry in a cloud of sizzle and steam.

8 ounces firm tofu, cut into 1/2-inch pieces

1/2 cup Asian Marinade (page 35)

1/4 teaspoon minced toasted chile de arbol (page 57)

1/2 teaspoon cornstarch

1 tablespoon rice vinegar

1 tablespoon lemon juice

1 tablespoon low-sodium soy sauce

1/2 teaspoon Asian sesame oil

6 scallions, sliced

1 red bell pepper, stemmed, seeded, and diced

1 teaspoon minced fresh ginger

1 large mango (about 8 ounces), peeled, seeded, and cut into
   1/4-inch-thick slices

1/2 teaspoon chopped fresh cilantro

2 cups cooked brown rice

Per Serving:

224 calories

6 g total fat (21% of calories)

1 g saturated fat

0 mg cholesterol

8 g protein (14% of calories)

38 g carbohydrates (65% of calories)

3 g fiber

217 mg sodium

Makes 4 servings

1. Preheat the oven to 375°F. Lightly spray a baking sheet or half-sheet pan with vegetable oil spray.

2. Put the tofu in a colander set over a bowl and refrigerate for at least 2 hours to drain. Discard the drained liquid and transfer the tofu to a glass or ceramic dish. Pour the marinade over the tofu, toss gently to coat, cover, and refrigerate for at least 2 hours more. Toss the tofu in the marinade once or twice during marinating.

3. Spread the tofu in a single layer on the baking sheet and bake for about 20 minutes, until golden brown. Take care not to overbake or the tofu will be tough—it should be al dente (see Note).

4. In a small bowl, mix the cornstarch with 2 tablespoons of water and stir until smooth. Add 1/2 cup plus 2 tablespoons water, the vinegar, lemon juice, soy sauce, and sesame oil and stir well.

5. Lightly spray a large sauté pan or wok with vegetable oil spray and heat over medium-high heat until hot. Add the scallion, red pepper, ginger, mango, and the tofu and stir-fry for 1 to 2 minutes. Add the cornstarch mixture and continue stir-frying for 2 to 3 minutes longer, until the sauce thickens and vegetables are fork-tender and heated through. Season with cilantro and serve over the rice.

NOTE: *To make sure the tofu is al dente when cooked, freeze it first. When ready to marinate, thaw and squeeze out the excess moisture before cutting. If you freeze it, there is no need to drain it in the refrigerator. Simply squeeze out the excess moisture and marinate it.*

Selecting and Preparing Tofu and Tempeh

Anyone who visits Rancho La Puerta quickly realizes that I frequently cook with tofu and tempeh. There is good reason for this: both are outstanding sources of protein and when you are committed to a vegetarian diet, they are close to essential. However, contrary to popular belief, neither is low in fat. A quarter pound of tofu has 85 calories, 9.5 grams of protein, and 5 grams of fat, of which all but half a gram is unsaturated. It also is a good source of fiber, potassium, and vitamins. This means tofu is healthful but not fat-free! There is low-fat tofu, which is very good, but it is not fat-free. A quarter pound of tempeh has about 200 calories, 16 grams of protein, and 4 grams of unsaturated fat. My advice when buying tofu and tempeh is read the nutritional data on the label.

Tofu is made from combining soy milk with a coagulant and compressing it into cakes. Generally about one pound in weight, it is packed in water and refrigerated. You can find tofu in the dairy section of the supermarket or in Asian markets, where it may be sold packaged or loose in tubs. Because tofu is often, but not always, used in place of dairy products, it is a boon to anyone with lactose intolerance.

Tofu may be extra firm, firm, or soft (silken). The soft tofus, in particular, may be flavored with herbs, much like cream cheese is flavored, although I prefer to flavor my own. I use the firmer tofus for cooking and the softer ones for desserts. Chinese-style tofus tend to be a little firmer than the more easy-to-find Japanese-style tofus, which are sold in supermarkets and health food stores. Look for Chinese-style tofu in Chinese and other Asian markets. Tofu should be stored covered with water and refrigerated for no longer than five days. Keep it in its original container or in a covered dish with plenty of fresh water.

When I marinate tofu, I first drain it. I prefer to drain it for at least four hours and up to eight, if possible. I put it in a colander, set the colander over a dish, and refrigerate the tofu. Refrigeration is important because this high-protein food should be treated as carefully as any other, such as fish or poultry, and never left at room temperature for too long. I do not weight the tofu as it drains—although some people suggest it—feeling that the weight alters the texture of the product. Once the tofu is drained, it can be marinated in any number of flavorful mixtures, although I generally prefer soy sauce–based marinades. For the best flavor, let the tofu marinate, again in the refrigerator, for about eight hours (overnight, or all day).

Tempeh, which comes to us from Southeast Asia, is made from fermented soy, rice, millet, or legumes. It is pressed into firm patties that usually weigh from four to eight ounces and are excellent for baking, grilling, sautéing, broiling, or braising. As with tofu, I marinate plain tempeh, which needs no draining and which attracts the flavors of the marinade very nicely. When tempeh is grilled or broiled, many people think it "tastes like meat." Whether this is important to you or not, tempeh is considered a great food for a vegetarian diet.

Ranch Pizzas

These little guys take time to put together but are really worth the effort. Experiment with your own favorite topping. At the Ranch, we favor using a base of pesto or tomato sauce, topped with chopped sun-dried tomatoes, zucchini, and a scant sprinkling of low-fat mozzarella.

3/4 cup warm water

1 tablespoon active dry yeast

1 teaspoon brown sugar or honey

1 teaspoon olive oil

1/2 teaspoon salt

1/4 teaspoon hot red pepper flakes

4 garlic cloves, minced

2 tablespoons chopped fresh basil

1 cup whole wheat flour

2 cups unbleached all-purpose flour

3 tablespoons Ranch Pesto (page 52) or Tomato-Basil Sauce (page 50)

1/4 cup rehydrated, chopped dry-packed sun-dried tomatoes (optional)

1 medium zucchini, thinly sliced (optional)

2 ounces low-fat mozzarella, goat cheese, or feta cheese (optional), grated or crumbled

Per Serving:

166 calories

4 g total fat (20% of calories)

1 g saturated fat

3 mg cholesterol

6 g protein (14% of calories)

28 g carbohydrates (66% of calories)

3 g fiber

152 mg sodium

Makes 12 servings

1. In a large mixing bowl, combine the warm water, yeast, and brown sugar. When the yeast dissolves and the mixture begins to bubble and foam, stir in the olive oil, salt, red pepper flakes, garlic, and basil. Using a wooden spoon, mix in the whole wheat flour. Work in the white flour, a little at a time, until the dough pulls away from the sides of the bowl.

2. Turn out onto a lightly floured surface and knead, adding more flour as needed, until your hands come clean (see Note). Continue kneading until the dough is smooth and elastic. Transfer to a bowl, cover with a towel, and set in a warm place for about 45 minutes, until doubled in volume.

3. Preheat the oven to 450°F.

4. Punch the dough down and knead for 2 to 3 minutes. Divide into 6 equal portions and form into balls. Using a rolling pin, roll each ball into a flat pizza round 6 to 8 inches in diameter and 1/8 inch thick.

5. Top each round with pesto or tomato sauce, sun-dried tomatoes, zucchini, and cheese, if desired. Set pizzas directly on the baking rack and bake for 8 to 15 minutes, or until the topping is hot and the cheese is golden. To serve, cut each pizza in half.

NOTE: *To test if the dough is well kneaded, insert a clean thumb into the dough and count to 5. If your thumb comes out clean, the dough is kneaded properly and you do not have to add any more flour.*

Mushroom–Potato Burgers

At home, these burgers are usually on my table the day after I make too many mashed potatoes, but don't always wait until you have leftovers. This delicious alternative to a high-fat hamburger stands on its own.

1/4 teaspoon olive oil

1/2 cup chopped onion

2 teaspoons minced garlic

1 cup sliced, stemmed white mushrooms

1/3 cup grated carrots

1 1/4 cups unseasoned mashed potatoes (from 2 large russets)

1 large egg white

2 tablespoons dry bread crumbs

2 tablespoons ground cashews

2 scallions, thinly sliced

1 1/2 teaspoons chopped fresh oregano or basil

1/2 teaspoon crushed toasted coriander seeds (see Note)

1/4 teaspoon minced fresh ginger

Pinch of hot red pepper flakes

Salt and freshly ground black pepper

1 tablespoon sesame seeds

1 tablespoon sunflower seeds

5 slices whole wheat bread

2 tablespoons Dijon mustard

1/2 head romaine lettuce, shredded

1 medium tomato, thinly sliced

1 red onion, thinly sliced

Per Serving:

209 calories

6 g total fat (25% of calories)

1 g saturated fat

1 mg cholesterol

8 g protein (15% of calories)

33 g carbohydrates (60% of calories)

5 g fiber

435 mg sodium

Makes 5 servings

1. In a medium sauté pan, heat the oil over medium heat and sauté the onion and garlic for about 5 minutes, until the onion is golden. Add the mushrooms and carrots and sauté for about 5 minutes longer, until the vegetables begin to soften. Drain any excess liquid and transfer the vegetables to a large bowl.

2. Add the potatoes, egg white, bread crumbs, cashews, scallion, oregano, coriander seeds, ginger, red pepper flakes, and salt and pepper to taste and mix well. The mixture will be moist.

3. In a small bowl, mix the sesame seeds with the sunflower seeds. On a flat dish or clean, dry work surface, spread the sesame seeds and sunflower seeds in a single layer. Use an ice cream scoop and scoop up a fifth of the potato mixture. Between dampened palms, flatten the mixture into a patty and coat on both sides with the seeds. Set aside on a waxed paper–lined tray while forming the other 4 patties.

4. Preheat a stovetop grill or heat a large sauté pan lightly sprayed with vegetable oil spray over medium heat. Cook the patties, turning once, for about 3 minutes on each side or until golden brown.

5. Toast the bread slices and spread 1 side of each slice with mustard. Top with lettuce, tomato, and onion and then with a burger. Serve immediately as open-faced sandwiches.

NOTE: *To toast coriander seeds, spread them in a dry skillet and cook over medium-high heat, shaking, for about 1 minute until fragrant. Transfer to a plate to cool.*

Grilled Vegetable Brochettes

La parilla (the grill) is a great way to cook a meal with little or no fat. Real mesquite charcoal is the fuel most often used in the Southwest and in Mexico. You can sometimes buy it in bags from a favorite restaurant, or search for it in gourmet shops. It imparts a smoky taste that is truly different from those chipped and formed briquettes, although they'll do in a pinch.

2 tablespoons balsamic vinegar

1 teaspoon low-sodium soy sauce

2 garlic cloves, minced

1 tablespoon chopped fresh basil

Freshly ground black pepper

4 portobello mushrooms, trimmed and stems reserved

2 yellow summer squash, trimmed and cut into 1/4-inch-thick slices

2 Japanese eggplants, trimmed and cut into 1/4-inch-thick slices

2 red onions, quartered

2 red bell peppers, stemmed, seeded, and quartered

8 scallions, trimmed and cut into 4-inch lengths

8 cherry tomatoes

Per Serving:

146 calories

2 g total fat (9% of calories)

0 g saturated fat

0 mg cholesterol

6 g protein (15% of calories)

33 g carbohydrates (76% of calories)

12 g fiber

111 mg sodium

Makes 4 servings

1. Prepare a charcoal or gas grill until the coals are medium-hot.

2. In a large glass or ceramic bowl, mix the vinegar, soy sauce, garlic, and basil and season to taste with pepper. Add the vegetables, including the mushroom stems, and toss to coat. Set aside to marinate at room temperature for about 10 minutes.

3. Thread 8 soaked bamboo skewers with the vegetables, reserving and setting aside the portobello mushroom caps. Begin each skewer with a mushroom stem. Arrange the vegetables on the skewers so that the colors are mixed.

4. Place the portobello caps and the skewers on the grill over medium-hot coals and grill for about 12 minutes, basting several times with the marinade. Turn the mushrooms and the skewers to grill evenly and make attractive grill marks on the mushrooms. Serve immediately.

Side Dishes

EVERY GREAT PLAY OR MOVIE'S MAIN CHARACTER *needs a supporting cast. At first, vegetable side dishes might seem like a meal's afterthought, but I disagree! I plan each meal's presentation, along with my sous chefs Rigo and Gonzalo, with an eye toward nutritional value, how flavors complement each other, and what's simple but pleasing to the eye. Here are some favorites.*

Rosemary Baked Potatoes

Having fragrant rosemary bushes surrounding my kitchens is an extra plus, but I actually started baking potatoes this way in the late 1970s, long before I arrived at the Ranch. The first chef I worked for was Luis Luzzati, who baked olive oil–rubbed potatoes on a bed of fresh rosemary and used foot-long rosemary sprigs to brush garlicky oil on nearly everything else. I don't use the oil anymore, but I haven't forsaken the rosemary.

8 sprigs fresh rosemary
4 russet potatoes, scrubbed

1. Preheat the oven to 350°F.

2. Lay the rosemary sprigs on a clean, dry baking sheet. Pierce the potatoes several times with the tines of a fork or a small, sharp knife and set on top of the rosemary, making sure 2 sprigs are under each potato. Bake for 45 to 60 minutes, until the potatoes are tender and cooked through. Serve hot.

Per Serving:

204 calories

0 g fat (3% of calories)

0 g saturated fat

0 mg cholesterol

3 g protein (10% of calories)

28 g carbohydrate (87% of calories)

2 g fiber

10 mg sodium

Makes 4 servings

Broccoli Potatoes

Mashed potatoes are a favorite comfort food. I add broccoli for both flavor and color without adding many calories and any fat; the buttermilk enhances the richness with just a little fat. Substitute cauliflower, zucchini, carrots, rutabaga, or roasted garlic for the broccoli, if you wish.

2 russet potatoes, peeled and quartered
1 cup peeled and sliced broccoli spears
1 garlic clove, minced
1 teaspoon chopped fresh oregano
1/2 cup low-fat buttermilk
Salt and freshly ground black pepper

1. In a large saucepan or stockpot, bring the potatoes and about 2 quarts water to a boil over medium-high. Reduce the heat and simmer, covered, for about 30 minutes or until the potatoes are soft enough to mash.

2. In a medium saucepan filled with water, cook the broccoli for 15 to 20 minutes, until soft. Drain, transfer to a food processor, and pulse until finely chopped.

3. Drain the potatoes and combine with the broccoli in a large bowl. Add the garlic, oregano, and buttermilk and mash with a fork or potato masher. Season to taste with salt and pepper and serve.

Per Serving:
56 calories
0 g total fat (5% of calories)
0 g saturated fat
1 mg cholesterol
2 g protein (16% of calories)
11 g carbohydrates (79% of calories)
1 g fiber
38 mg sodium
Makes 6 servings

Braised Sliced Potatoes

4 russet potatoes

3 garlic cloves, minced

1 1/2 teaspoons minced fresh rosemary

1/4 teaspoon hot red pepper flakes, or 1/4 teaspoon crumbled toasted chile de arbol (page 57)

Salt and freshly ground white pepper

1/2 cup Basic Vegetable Stock (page 75) or water

Per Serving:

150 calories

0 g total fat (1% of calories)

0 g saturated fat

0 mg cholesterol

3 g protein (8% of calories)

34 g carbohydrates (91% of calories)

1 g fiber

12 mg sodium

Makes 6 servings

1. Preheat the oven to 375°F. Lightly spray an 8 by 8-inch baking pan with vegetable oil spray.

2. Cut the potatoes crosswise into 1/4-inch-thick slices, not cutting all the way through; the slices should still be attached at the base so that the potatoes appear whole.

3. Carefully arrange the potatoes end-to-end in the pan. Sprinkle with the garlic, rosemary, red pepper flakes, and salt and pepper to taste and pour the stock into the bottom of the pan. Cover with foil and bake for about 1 hour and 15 minutes, until the potatoes are tender.

4. Serve immediately, slicing through the potatoes and serving the slices, not the whole potatoes.

Eggplant-Potato Ratatouille

I am lucky to have an expansive organic garden that produces so many glorious vegetables. In this recipe, everything but the spices, salt, and mushrooms come from the Ranch's gardens. The dish stands by itself as a side, but if you add a little cooked rice or Kashi Breakfast Pilaf (page 131), it becomes a main course. I also like to toss in a few sun-dried tomatoes for richer flavor. While it is cooking, the simmering vegetables, herbs, star anise, and curry produce an enticing aroma, perfect for whetting the appetite.

Per Serving:

91 calories

1 g total fat (11% of calories)

0 g saturated fat

0 mg cholesterol

4 g protein (15% of calories)

19 g carbohydrates (74% of calories)

6 g fiber

199 mg sodium

Makes 6 servings

2 medium onions, chopped

1 russet potato, diced

1 carrot, diced

1 medium eggplant, trimmed and cut into 1/2-inch-thick cubes

1 large zucchini, diced

1 medium tomato, chopped

1 red bell pepper, stemmed, seeded, and chopped

1/2 pound white mushrooms, trimmed and halved or quartered, depending on size

2 tablespoons minced garlic

1 teaspoon chopped fresh oregano

1/2 teaspoon chopped fresh thyme

Pinch of ground allspice

3 star anise

1 tablespoon curry powder

1 cup Basic Vegetable Stock (page 75)

Sea salt

1. Lightly spray a large sauté pan with vegetable spray and heat over medium-high heat. Add the onion, potato, and carrot and sauté for about 5 minutes, until onion is golden.

2. Add the eggplant, zucchini, tomato, red pepper, mushroom, and garlic and stir to mix. Season with oregano, thyme, and allspice, stirring gently. Add the star anise, curry powder, and stock and season to taste with salt.

3. Reduce the heat to low and simmer, covered, for about 25 minutes, until the vegetables soften. Set aside for about 10 minutes to allow the flavors to blend and develop. Remove the star anise and adjust the seasoning before serving.

Taking the Ranch Home

Everywhere you turn at Rancho La Puerta, someone is stretching. That group over by the sycamore tree just returned from the mountain hike? Stretching. A cluster of figures in the open-air gym, each flexing like grass in the wind? Stretching.

Three key muscles should be stretched every day: pectorals, hamstrings, and hip flexors. Ask an exercise professional to demonstrate if you're unfamiliar with the three basic movements described below, or if you are having any difficulty or pain doing them. Hold for 10 to 30 seconds. They're simple, yet wonderful!

Pectorals. Clasp your hands behind your back or above your head, give a big stretch, yawn, and lift your chest.

Hamstrings. Very important! Your lower back is much more relaxed when you keep these muscles flexible. Place one foot in front of the other, a little more than shoulder width. Keeping your front leg straight—heel on floor, foot lifted—bend the back knee, placing both hands on this knee and supporting some of your weight. Do a flat-back bow from the hip (the best you can!) over the straight leg and hold at least 10 seconds, 20 if possible.

Hip flexors. Our most-used muscle group, but the least stretched! They contract when you're sitting. To stretch, stand and put one foot forward, one foot back. Bend front knee, keeping shin vertical. Bend back knee with toe on ground and heel off until the thigh of your back leg is vertical with the body. Squeeze the buttocks very tight as you bring the hips forward and raise the chest, feeling the stretch in the rear leg and hip. (Basically, think of being upright from hips to shoulders, but with legs bent, front and back.) Hold the back of a chair placed to the side if you have difficulty balancing.

Green and Yellow Beans with Tomatoes

When the young tender string beans are in season, this is a dish I love to make. They are so sweet and tasty and cook right up in a flash.

1 onion, cut julienne

3 cloves fresh garlic, minced

2 tomatoes, chopped

1 teaspoon allspice

1 small pinch ground cloves

1/2 pound green string beans, trimmed and washed

1/2 pound yellow string beans, trimmed and washed

2 cups Basic Vegetable Stock (page 75)

1 tablespoon fresh oregano, chopped

Salt and freshly ground black pepper, to taste

Trim the ends off the beans and cut the beans in half on the bias. Set aside. In a sauté pan over medium heat, sauté the onion for 5 minutes. Add the garlic and tomato and cook, stirring, 5 minutes. Reduce the heat, add the remaining ingredients, and simmer for 10 minutes, covered. Let rest for 5 minutes, covered. Season to taste and enjoy.

Per Serving:

48 calories

1 g total fat (9% of calories)

0 g saturated fat

0 mg cholesterol

2 g protein (16% of calories)

11 g carbohydrates (75% of calories)

4 g fiber

107 mg sodium

Makes 6 servings

Red Yams with Oranges

Bright orange-red yams are low in calories and full of vitamin A and potassium, which leads some to claim that the yam and the sweet potato are pretty close to being perfect foods. And they're not far wrong. I use yams here because drier sweet potatoes tend to become mealy while the yams stay moist, creamy and so good! Of course, both tubers are, botanically speaking, sweet potatoes. True yams are larger and not available in the U.S. and environs.

2 yams, trimmed and halved lengthwise
2 cups fresh orange juice
1/2 teaspoon ground cinnamon
1/2 teaspoon vanilla extract
1 orange, thinly sliced

1. Preheat the oven to 375°F.

2. In a small bowl, combine the orange juice, cinnamon, and vanilla and stir well.

3. Arrange the yams in an ovenproof dish and pour the orange juice mixture over them. Lay the orange slices over the yams. Cover and bake for about 50 minutes, until soft. Serve hot or cold.

Per Serving:
160 calories
0 g total fat (2% of calories)
0 g saturated fat
0 mg cholesterol
2 g protein (8% of calories)
38 g carbohydrates (90% of calories)
4 g fiber
8 mg sodium
Makes 4 servings

Chile Carrots with Garlic

This may seem a bit garlicky when you read the amounts, but the wallop provided by the little bulb perfectly offsets the oregano and jalapeños. Carrots are a much-loved appetizer in Mexico, and big batches of these vinegary beauties often reside on counters or restaurant tables.

5 carrots, sliced 1/4 inch thick

2 medium onions, sliced 1/4 inch thick

6 garlic cloves, minced

2 tablespoons chopped fresh oregano

2 pickled jalapeño peppers, quartered

1 teaspoon olive oil

1/4 cup white wine vinegar

1/4 teaspoon freshly ground black pepper

2 bay leaves

In a pot of boiling water, blanch the carrots for about 30 seconds and drain. Transfer to a bowl, add the remaining ingredients, and toss well. Cover and refrigerate for at least 30 minutes or store for up to 6 days. Remove bay leaves before serving.

Per Serving:

38 calories

1 g fat (17% of calories)

0 g saturated fat

0 mg cholesterol

1 g protein (10% of calories)

8 g carbohydrate (73% of calories)

2 g fiber

521 mg sodium

Makes 10 servings

Mashed Parsnips with Leeks

Who'd think that a parsnip dish would generate so many recipe requests? This one surely does whenever I serve it to guests. Perhaps it's because many of us are wary of parsnips at first. White carrots? But, once they are cooked, a bite of their creamy, smooth texture usually means love ever after. Choose small, firm parsnips, as the large ones can have woody centers.

4 parsnips, peeled and cut into 2-inch-thick pieces
1/2 teaspoon olive oil
2 leeks, washed, trimmed, and cut into 2-inch julienne
1 carrot, diced
1 broccoli spear, peeled and diced
1 teaspoon low-sodium soy sauce
Freshly ground black pepper

1. In a large saucepan, combine the parsnips with enough water to cover by 1 or 2 inches. Bring to a simmer over medium heat and simmer for 25 to 30 minutes, until the parsnips are tender. Drain and set aside.

2. Heat the olive oil in a sauté pan over medium heat. Add the leeks and sauté for about 10 minutes, until the leeks are golden. Add the carrot, broccoli, soy sauce, and pepper to taste and cook for 2 or 3 minutes longer. Set aside.

3. Transfer the parsnips to a food processor and process until the parsnips are a smooth puree. Scrape into a bowl and fold in the sautéed vegetables. Season to taste and serve.

Per Serving:
108 calories
1 g total fat (7% of calories)
0 g saturated fat
0 mg cholesterol
3 g protein (9% of calories)
25 g carbohydrates (84% of calories)
6 g fiber
78 mg sodium
Makes 6 servings

Beets and Carrots with Fennel and Leeks

Beets, carrots, and fennel? You bet! This is a great marriage. The fennel delivers a special anise tang that, when combined with the sweetness of the beets and carrots, is a real flavor plus. This makes a great side dish or can be served as a salad.

4 medium (about 3/4 pound) beets with greens, bottoms peeled and chopped, greens coarsely chopped and reserved
1/2 teaspoon ground ginger
2 leeks, washed well and trimmed
2 fennel bulbs, trimmed
1/2 teaspoon olive oil
1 tablespoon low-sodium soy sauce
Freshly ground black pepper

1. In a large saucepan, combine the beets with enough cold water to cover by several inches, add the ginger, and bring to a boil over medium-high heat. Reduce the heat and simmer for about 15 minutes, until the beets are fork-tender. Strain and set aside.

2. Cut off and discard the green part of the leeks. Cut the white parts on the diagonal into thin slices and transfer to a bowl half-filled with cold water. Let the leeks soak for a few minutes, drain, and repeat to clean them thoroughly.

3. Cut the fennel bulbs in half and then into 1/4-inch-thick julienne. Transfer to a bowl half-filled with cold water and let the fennel soak for a few minutes. Drain.

4. In a large sauté pan, heat the oil over medium heat and sauté the leeks and fennel for 4 or 5 minutes, until golden brown. Add the reserved beet greens and the soy sauce and cook for 2 or 3 minutes longer, until the greens wilt. Add the beets and cook for a few minutes or until heated through. Season to taste generously with pepper and serve.

Per Serving:
58 calories
1 g total fat (8% of calories)
0 g saturated fat
0 mg cholesterol
2 g protein (12% of calories)
13 g carbohydrates (80% of calories)
2 g fiber
132 mg sodium
Makes 8 servings

Beets with Ginger and Lime

Ranch gardeners grow three or four varieties of beets every year: red, purple, red-and-white candy-striped, and brilliant golden ones. All are sweet and savory, and when tossed with a subtle vinaigrette, they don't lose their delicate flavor.

4 medium beets (about 3/4 pound), trimmed, greens saved for another
 purpose
1 medium onion, coarsely chopped
2 tablespoons rice vinegar
2 tablespoons fresh lime juice
2 teaspoons minced fresh ginger
1 teaspoon minced fresh oregano, or 1/4 teaspoon dried
Freshly ground black pepper

1. In a large saucepan, bring about a quart of water to a boil. Add the beets and onion, reduce the heat, and simmer for about 25 minutes, until the beets are fork-tender. Drain and peel the beets while holding them under cold running water; the skins will slip off. Discard the onion.

2. Cut the beets into 1/4-inch-thick slices and transfer to a large bowl. Add the vinegar, lime juice, ginger, and oregano and toss gently. Season to taste with pepper and serve warm or chilled.

Per Serving:
56 calories
0 g total fat (3% of calories)
0 g saturated fat
0 mg cholesterol
2 g protein (12% of calories)
12 g carbohydrates (85% of calories)
1 g fiber
62 mg sodium
Makes 4 servings

Cauliflower with Mustard Vinaigrette

Adding two tablespoons nonfat yogurt to the vinegars before tossing with the hot cauliflower gives the dish a creamy richness.

1 teaspoon balsamic vinegar
1 tablespoon coarse-grain Dijon mustard
1/4 teaspoon low-sodium soy sauce
1 head cauliflower, trimmed and cut into florets
1-inch piece fresh ginger, cut into 1/4-inch-thick slices
3 tablespoons fresh lime juice

1. In a small mixing bowl, combine the vinegar, mustard, and soy sauce and mix well.

2. In a large saucepan, bring about a quart of water to a boil. Add the cauliflower florets, ginger, and lime juice, reduce the heat, and simmer for about 25 minutes, until the florets are fork-tender. Drain and while still hot, toss with the vinegar-mustard mixture and serve.

Per Serving:
30 calories
0 g total fat (9% of calories)
0 g saturated fat
0 mg cholesterol
2 g protein (24% of calories)
5 g carbohydrates (67% of calories)
1 g fiber
51 mg sodium
Makes 6 servings

Bok Choy, Fennel, and Spinach

The fennel lends a clean anise flavor to this dish. It's great as a side dish, or even as a light entree when spooned over rice or cellophane noodles.

1 teaspoon Asian sesame oil

3 garlic cloves, thinly sliced

1 Thai chile or other dried hot chile

1 head bok choy, trimmed and sliced into 8 pieces

4 leeks, washed, trimmed, and sliced thinly on the bias (white part only)

2 fennel bulbs, trimmed and cut into 1/4-inch-thick slices

2 cups fresh spinach, washed well and tough stems discarded

1 star anise

1 teaspoon minced fresh ginger

1/2 cup Basic Vegetable Stock (page 75)

1/4 teaspoon chopped fresh rosemary

Low-sodium soy sauce

1. In a large sauté pan, heat the oil over medium heat. Add the garlic, chile, bok choy, and leeks and sauté for 3 or 4 minutes, until the leeks are golden.

2. Add the fennel, spinach, star anise, ginger, and stock. Reduce the heat and simmer for about 5 minutes, until the spinach wilts. Add the rosemary and season to taste with soy sauce. Discard the star anise and the chile. Serve hot.

Per Serving:

141 calories

2 g total fat (13% of calories)

0 g saturated fat

0 mg cholesterol

5 g protein (12% of calories)

29 g carbohydrates (75% of calories)

4 g fiber

121 mg sodium

Makes 4 servings

NOTE: *Wash both the leeks and bok choy very carefully, as dirt and grit can be trapped in the folds of these vegetables.*

Spinach with Garlic and Sautéed Onions

Originally from southwestern Asia, spinach is an herbaceous annual that conquered the cooking world from China to Europe. The Moors introduced it to Spain in the eighth century. I find the rich, deep green hue of this gently cooked spinach is also a perfect partner for tofu, tempeh, and pasta.

1/2 teaspoon olive oil
1/2 medium onion, chopped
4 garlic cloves, chopped
2 pounds fresh spinach, washed well and chopped, tough stems discarded
1 teaspoon balsamic vinegar
Freshly ground black pepper

In a large sauté pan, heat the oil over medium-high heat and sauté the onion for about 3 minutes, until golden. Add the garlic and sauté for about 2 minutes, until softened. Add the spinach and stir for about 2 minutes, until the spinach starts to wilt. Add the vinegar and pepper to taste, tossing to mix. Serve immediately while still hot.

Per Serving:

32 calories

1 g total fat (16% of calories)

0 g saturated fat

0 mg cholesterol

3 g protein (35% of calories)

5% of carbohydrates (49% of calories)

3 g fiber

124 mg sodium

Makes 8 servings

Jicama With Broccoli

If you're new to sliced raw jicama, you may not be able to place it. Some Ranch guests think it's a cold fried potato, yet they're baffled by its crunchiness. Even in the kitchen, this dish is a favorite snack. We set out a plate of sliced jicama bathed in fresh lime juice, dusted with hot chile powder, and surrounded by slices of orange, grapefruit, and cucumber. Sometimes we add thinly sliced red onions that have been briefly marinated in lime juice—about five minutes.

1 jicama (about 1 pound), peeled and cut into julienne
2 garlic cloves, minced
1 teaspoon minced fresh ginger
1 red bell pepper, stemmed, seeded, and chopped
2 cups broccoli florets (about a 6-ounce crown)
1/2 cup fresh lime juice (juice of 3 limes)
1/3 cup fresh orange juice (juice of 1 orange)
1 teaspoon low-sodium soy sauce
1/4 teaspoon hot red pepper flakes
1 tablespoon chopped fresh cilantro

1. Lightly spray a large sauté pan with vegetable oil spray and sauté the jicama for about 1 minute. Add the garlic and ginger, and sauté for about 2 minutes, until the jicama starts to soften.

2. Add the red pepper, broccoli, lime and orange juice, soy sauce, and red pepper flakes and cook for 2 to 3 minutes, until the broccoli turns bright green. Serve hot, sprinkled with cilantro.

Per Serving:
103 calories
0 g total fat (4% of calories)
0 g saturated fat
0 mg cholesterol
3 g protein (13% of calories)
21 g carbohydrates (83% of calories)
2 g fiber
53 mg sodium
Makes 4 servings

Taking the Ranch Home

Posture is everything! Most people are aware posture is important when they exercise, but so often they forget about it while doing day-to-day things—sitting in the car, at a desk, eating a meal, looking around, talking with a friend. Then, suddenly, the body goes into every variety of slouch and slant.

Be mindful of how you sit and stand, at rest or on the go. Good posture can offset a great number of chronic tension problems in the back, hip, neck, and shoulders. Straighten the back, stretch the head and neck vertically, drop the shoulders, and bring the shoulder blades closer together. Now even your mother can't launch into a harangue about standing up straight.

Mexican Black and Pinto Beans

I love beans and often make a meal of rice and beans. This recipe is tasty and so healthy. You can serve it hot with an entree or alone, or as a cold salad. Or mash the beans and spread them on a tostada.

1/2 cup black beans, sorted and
  rinsed

1/2 cup pinto beans, sorted and
  rinsed

6 cups Basic Vegetable Stock (page
  75) or water, plus more if needed

1 medium onion, diced

1 medium tomato, diced

1 poblano chile, stemmed, seeded,
  and chopped

1 chile de arbol, stemmed, seeded,
  and chopped

3 garlic cloves, minced

2 tablespoons chopped fresh oregano

1/2 teaspoon freshly ground black
  pepper

Salt

1 tablespoon chopped fresh cilantro

1/4 cup crumbled feta cheese

Per Serving:

55 calories

1 g total fat (20% of calories)

1 g saturated fat

4 mg cholesterol

3 g protein (20% of calories)

8 g carbohydrates (60% of calories)

1 g fiber

126 mg sodium

Makes 8 servings

1. Put the beans in a large bowl and add about 10 cups of water. Soak for at least 8 hours or overnight, changing the water a few times, if possible. Drain and transfer to a stockpot.

2. Add the stock, onion, tomato, chiles, garlic, 1 tablespoon of oregano and the pepper. Season to taste with salt and bring to a boil over high heat. Reduce the heat and simmer, covered, for about 1 hour and 20 minutes or until the beans are soft, with the texture of a baked potato. (A good test for doneness is to pinch a bean between your thumb and forefinger to test the consistency.)

3. Serve the beans hot or cold, garnished with the remaining tablespoon of oregano, the cilantro, and feta cheese.

Barbecued Fava Beans, Tecate Style

In Mexico, if you invite a family to come for a little barbecue, be prepared for a crowd. Mexicans love to party. Case in point: I once returned home a little late for my own casual get-together with Rigo from the Ranch kitchen and his family. About twenty cars crowded my driveway and were lined up along the road. Smoke and delicious smells poured from my back-yard, where scallions, jalapeño peppers, and fava beans, still in the pod, fought for space on the grill.

20 fava bean pods (see Note)
8 large scallions, trimmed and left whole
4 large jalapeño peppers
1/4 cup low-sodium soy sauce
Juice of 2 limes
Salt

1. Prepare a charcoal or gas grill.

2. Lay the fava bean pods, scallions, and jalapeños on the grill away from the most intense heat. Grill slowly over this indirect heat for 10 to 15 minutes, turning with tongs several times until pods are slightly charred and scallions are tender. The scallions may not take as long as the pods and jalapeños. Remove from the grill and arrange on a plate.

3. Serve immediately, with soy sauce, lime juice, and salt sprinkled over them. Peel the pods and remove the beans before eating.

Per Serving:

84 calories
0.5 g total fat (4% of calories)
0.1 g saturated fat
0 mg cholesterol
5 g protein (18% of calories)
20 g carbohydrates (78% of calories)
6 g fiber
861 mg sodium

Makes 4 servings

NOTE: *Fava beans resemble large, beige lima beans and, for a short time in the spring, are available fresh in the pods, which are long and fairly flat. Fava beans are also called broad beans.*

White Beans With Aromatic Herbs

Slow oven cooking allows the beans to absorb all of their surrounding fla-
vors. This dish is similar to the cassoulets I used to make in my "other"
culinary life, but I no longer put in the goose fat and wine! Don't worry...
you won't miss them. Serve these beans with bread and a salad and you've
made a hearty meal of it. If you live in a high-altitude hard-water area,
increase the cooking time.

Per Serving:

267 calories

2 g total fat (6% of calories)

0 g saturated fat

0 mg cholesterol

15 g protein (21% of calories)

51 g carbohydrates (73% of calories)

2 g fiber

435 mg sodium

Makes 6 servings

2 cups great northern beans, rinsed and sorted

1/2 teaspoon olive oil

1 medium onion, chopped

1 carrot, diced

1 celery rib, diced

4 garlic cloves, chopped

1 all-purpose potato, peeled and diced

4 cups Basic Vegetable Stock (page 75)

2 bay leaves

2 sprigs fresh thyme

2 sprigs fresh oregano

1 sprig fresh rosemary

1 tablespoon maple syrup

1 teaspoon sea salt

1/2 teaspoon freshly ground black

1. Put the beans in a large bowl and add about 10 cups of water. Soak for at least 8 hours or overnight, changing the water a few times, if possible. Drain and transfer to a stockpot.

2. In a stockpot, heat the oil over medium-high heat. Add the onion, carrot, and celery and sauté for about 5 minutes, until the onion is golden. Add the garlic and potato, and sauté for about 2 minutes, until the garlic softens. Add the beans, stock, bay leaves, herb sprigs, maple syrup, salt, and pepper and stir to mix. Reduce the heat and simmer for about 20 minutes, until the flavors blend and the beans begin to soften.

3. Preheat the oven to 350°F. Lightly spray a 2-quart casserole or baking dish with vegetable oil spray.

4. Transfer the bean mixture to the casserole, cover, and bake for about 1 1/2 hours, until the beans are silken and soft. Set aside for about 15 minutes to cool and for the flavors to blend. Serve immediately.

Mexican Rice with Tomatoes

This is a healthful way to prepare Mexican rice—fast, easy, and delicious. The traditional Mexican method of frying the vegetables and rice in oil and using heavily salted chicken stock isn't used here, so the fat and calories are much lower than expected.

1/2 teaspoon olive oil

1/2 medium onion, diced

1/2 carrot, diced

2 garlic cloves, minced

1 cup brown rice

1/2 medium tomato, chopped

1/2 jalapeño pepper, minced

3 cups Basic Vegetable Stock (page 75) or water

1 tablespoon chopped fresh cilantro

1/2 teaspoon salt, or to taste

1. Preheat the oven to 350°F.

2. In a large sauté pan, ovenproof dish, or casserole, heat the oil over medium heat and sauté the onion, carrot, and garlic for 2 to 3 minutes. Add the rice and continue to cook, stirring for 2 minutes, to coat the rice with oil and vegetables. Add the tomato, jalapeño, and stock and cook, stirring and scraping the sides of the pan, until well mixed. Add the cilantro and salt.

3. Cover and bake for about 30 minutes. Remove from the oven and let stand, covered, for 5 to 6 minutes to set. Uncover and test for doneness. If the liquid is not absorbed and the rice cooked, cover and return to the oven for a few minutes longer, until done.

Per Serving:

99 calories

1 g total fat (9% of calories)

0 g saturated fat

0 mg cholesterol

2 g protein (9% of calories)

20 g carbohydrates (82% of calories)

1 g fiber

41 mg sodium

Makes 8 servings

NOTE: *To cook on top of the stove, simmer, covered, over low heat for 25 to 30 minutes. Set aside to set for 5 to 6 minutes and then test for doneness. For green tomatillo rice, substitute 1/2 cup Rosie's Z-Wah Tomatillo Salsa (page 45) for the tomato and add 1/4 cup of corn kernels.*

Wild Rice, Cranberries, and Oranges

Actually a native American grass, wild rice deserves to move off the Thanksgiving table and into meals at any time of year. Bright red cranberries and orange sections give this a festive look, but don't stop there—substitute cherries or apricots. Be careful not to overcook the wild rice; it should be tender, but still have some of its unique crunchiness.

1 cup wild rice
1 medium onion, minced
1 tablespoon low-sodium soy sauce
1 tablespoon rice vinegar
1/2 teaspoon minced fresh ginger
1/2 teaspoon minced garlic
2 scallions, trimmed and sliced on the bias
1 navel orange, peeled and sectioned
1/2 cup dried cranberries

1. Rinse the rice in a colander or sieve and set aside to drain.

2. Lightly spray a large saucepan with vegetable oil spray and heat over medium heat. Add the onion and cook, stirring, for about 30 seconds. Add the rice, 4 cups water, soy sauce, vinegar, ginger, and garlic. Reduce the heat and simmer, covered, for 40 to 45 minutes, until the rice is al dente. Do not overcook.

3. Stir in the scallions, orange segments, and cranberries and set aside for about 5 minutes to give the berries a chance to soften slightly. Serve immediately.

Per Serving:

222 calories

1 g total fat (2% of calories)

0 g saturated fat

0 mg cholesterol

8 g protein (13% of calories)

50 g carbohydrates (85% of calories)

6 g fiber

271 mg sodium

Makes 4 servings

Taking the Ranch Home

Nature is always an unfailing source of inspiration. Many guests come to the ranch primarily because it's in the midst of nature. Even the landscaping is a colorful palette of native plants and Mediterranean-climate sages. When you're at home again, step outside at every opportunity. Escape the catacombs of an office building. Discover a small patio or plaza where light filters down through a tree. You need a sense of escape, a chance to breathe deep and look around and within you.

Greek Rice with Feta

While sailing from one island to another in the eastern Mediterranean one summer, I ate at many small cafés, but one, on Mykonos, stands out in my memory. The food was superb, and a simple lemon-scented rice served with the dolmas was perfect. When I returned home I had to duplicate it. This is it. For extra flavor, add some Moroccan Lemons (page 61).

1/2 teaspoon olive oil
1 medium onion, diced
3 garlic cloves, sliced
1 cup brown rice
3 cups Basic Vegetable Stock (page 75)
Salt
Juice and grated zest of 1 lemon
2 tablespoons crumbled feta cheese
1 scallion, sliced
1 tablespoon chopped fresh cilantro

1. In a deep sauté pan or saucepan, heat the oil over medium heat and sauté the onion and garlic for 2 or 3 minutes. Add the rice and continue cooking, stirring, for 2 minutes, until coated with oil. Add the stock, stirring and scraping the sides of the pan, until the rice is cooked. Season to taste with salt.

2. Cover and simmer over low heat for 25 to 30 minutes. Set aside, covered, to steam for 5 or 6 minutes. Uncover and test for doneness. If the liquid is not absorbed and the rice is tender, return the pan to the stove for a few minutes.

3. Add the feta, scallion, and cilantro and stir gently just until mixed. Serve immediately.

Per Serving:
104 calories
1 g total fat (12% of calories)
0 g saturated fat
2 mg cholesterol
3 g protein (9% of calories)
22 g carbohydrate (79% of calories)
0 g fiber
93 mg sodium
Makes 8 servings

Curried Quinoa Tabbouleh with Tofu

Substituting this ancient Andean grain for classic bulgur wheat adds a slightly different nutty (but clean, not oily) flavor and a crunchy toothiness to a classic Middle Eastern dish. Quinoa is close to done when the grains start looking slightly transparent.

1 cup quinoa, rinsed and drained

1 tablespoon low-sodium soy sauce

1 tablespoon curry powder

1 teaspoon minced garlic

1/4 pound firm tofu, cut into 1/4-inch-thick pieces

2 cups minced flat-leaf parsley

1 medium tomato, diced

1 medium cucumber, peeled and diced

1 scallion, trimmed and diced

2 tablespoons fresh lime juice

1 tablespoon chopped fresh mint

Sea salt and freshly ground black pepper

6 large red leaf lettuce leaves

1 head romaine lettuce, chopped

Per Serving:

222 calories

5 g total fat (17% of calories)

1 g saturated fat

0 mg cholesterol

14 g protein (22% of calories)

37 g carbohydrates (61% of calories)

8 g fiber

197 mg sodium

Makes 6 servings

1. In a saucepan, combine the quinoa, 5 cups water, soy sauce, curry powder, and garlic and bring to a boil over medium-high heat. Reduce the heat and simmer for about 15 minutes, until the quinoa is tender and appears transparent. Set aside to cool.

2. Drain the quinoa in a sieve. Transfer to a large bowl and add the tofu, parsley, tomato, cucumber, scallion, lime juice, and mint. Toss well, fluffing the grains, and season to taste with salt and pepper.

3. Arrange the red leaf lettuce leaves on 6 plates and top with the chopped romaine lettuce. Spoon the tabbouleh over the lettuce and serve immediately.

Desserts

LOOKING NERVOUSLY OVER YOUR SHOULDER *for the calorie police? Have no fear. You can plunder in pleasurable low-calorie splendor here. I never use butter, lard, margarine, or high-fat dairy products in my recipes, yet the kitchen gets high fives on our desserts every week. From the low-fat but creamy cheesecakes and sweet potato pie to the crunchy postre del sol and our ever-popular biscotti, there are always plenty of desserts to satisfy a craving for sweets.*

Although these desserts can stand on their own merits, a couple of spoonsful of fruit sauces will add flavor and brilliant colors. These pure fruit sauces are made from the freshest of the fresh, and you can use them frequently, even lavishly, with no calorie or fat worries. We have made double portions of the banana, papaya, guava, and orange fruit sauces ever since guests discovered they can do a little "bartending" with them. They spoon one of these sauces into a glass with some ice to make a smoothie, and slurp it down like there's no tomorrow.

I choose the ripest, unblemished fruit in season, and taste it before using. When natural sugars are allowed to develop in fruit naturally, rather than in a boat hold or warehouse, they have a flavor that's never "off." I also make a nonfat chocolate sauce that's very low in calories. Try it over frozen bananas.

Banana-Oatmeal Cookies

These little guys are always a big hit at the Ranch, with little and big kids alike. We always serve these during Kids' Week, but guests request them during our grown-up weeks, too.

1 cup unbleached all-purpose flour
3/4 cup old-fashioned rolled oats
1/4 cup chopped walnuts or pecans
1/2 teaspoon baking powder
1/3 teaspoon baking soda
1/2 teaspoon salt
1/2 cup packed light or dark brown sugar

1/3 cup canola oil margarine (see Note)
2 large egg whites
1/3 cup mashed bananas
1/4 teaspoon vanilla extract
1/4 teaspoon fresh lemon juice

Per Cookie:

39 calories
2 g total fat (45% of calories)
0 g saturated fat
0 mg cholesterol
1 g protein (7% of calories)
5 g carbohydrates (47% of calories)
0 g fiber
59 mg sodium

Makes 30 cookies

NOTE: *Canola margarine does not process like saturated or other hydrogenated fats and so will not produce a creamy or fluffy batter.*

1. Preheat the oven to 350°F. Lightly spray a cookie sheet with vegetable oil spray.

2. In a large bowl, combine the flour, oats, walnuts, baking powder, baking soda, and salt and whisk 8 or 9 times to aerate and mix.

3. In the bowl of an electric mixer set on medium, mix the brown sugar and margarine until the mixture is crumbly. Beat in the egg whites, bananas, vanilla, and lemon juice.

4. Pour the wet ingredients into the dry ingredients and stir with a wooden spoon until well combined. Drop by heaping tablespoonfuls onto the cookie sheets, leaving about an inch between each, and bake for 15 to 18 minutes, or until golden. Cool on the sheets for about 5 minutes before transferring to wire racks to cool.

Amazing Cookies

I make a double or triple batch because these go fast, and I freeze the ones that survive the first onslaught for those sweet-tooth emergencies later on. Figure an additional 7 calories in each cookie if you add the chocolate chips. I do.

3/4 cup whole wheat pastry flour

1 cup old-fashioned rolled oats

1 1/2 teaspoons ground cinnamon

1/2 teaspoon baking soda

2 bananas

2 large egg whites

2 tablespoons light or dark brown sugar

2 1/4 teaspoons grated orange zest

1 teaspoon vanilla extract

1/4 teaspoon orange extract

3/4 cup raisins

1/4 cup semisweet chocolate chips (optional)

Per Cookie:

45 calories

0 g total fat (6% of calories)

0 g saturated fat

0 mg cholesterol

1 g protein (11% of calories)

9 g carbohydrates (83% of calories)

0 g fiber

18 mg sodium

Makes 30 cookies

1. Preheat the oven to 350°F. Lightly spray 2 cookie sheets with vegetable oil spray.

2. In a large mixing bowl, combine the flour, oats, cinnamon, and baking soda and whisk 8 or 9 times until well mixed.

3. In a food processor or blender, combine the bananas, egg whites, brown sugar, orange zest, and vanilla and orange extracts and process until smooth and creamy.

4. Fold the wet ingredients into the dry ingredients. Fold in the raisins and, if desired, the chocolate chips. Drop the dough by rounded tablespoons onto the baking sheets, leaving about 1 inch between them, and bake for about 10 minutes, or until lightly browned on the bottom. Cool completely on wire racks.

Biscotti with Fennel Seeds

This is a delicious low-fat way to satisfy your sweet tooth. Serve these with fruit butter and seasonal fruit.

BISCOTTI

2 cups whole wheat pastry flour
2 teaspoons baking powder
1/4 teaspoon salt
6 large egg whites
1/2 cup packed light or dark brown sugar
1 teaspoon vanilla extract
1 teaspoon almond extract
2 tablespoons canola oil
1 tablespoon fennel seeds, toasted
1/4 cup ground almonds
1 tablespoon grated orange zest

GLAZE

2 tablespoons packed light or dark brown sugar
1 tablespoon ground cinnamon

1. Preheat the oven to 325°F. Lightly spray 2 cookie sheets with vegetable oil spray.

2. To make the biscotti, in a large bowl, combine the flour, baking powder, and salt and whisk 7 or 8 times to aerate and mix.

Per 2 Cookies:

103 calories

3 g total fat (24% of calories)

0 g saturated fat

0 mg cholesterol

2 g protein (12% of calories)

17 g carbohydrates (64% of calories)

0 g fiber

91 mg sodium

Makes 36 cookies

3. In the bowl of an electric mixer set on medium-high speed or using a balloon whisk, beat the egg whites and brown sugar until creamy. Fold in the vanilla and almond extracts and then quickly fold the dry ingredients into the whites and sugar mixture. Add the oil, fennel seeds, almonds, and zest and stir until blended and is a thick dough.

4. Turn out onto a well-floured work surface and divide the dough into quarters. With floured hands, roll each into a cylinder that is approximately 3 inches in diameter. Transfer the rolls to the cookie sheets. Using a small, sharp knife, cut a thin, lengthwise slash about 1/4 inch deep down the center of each roll.

5. To make the glaze, in a small bowl, mix the brown sugar and cinnamon and sprinkle evenly over the top of the rolls.

6. Bake for 25 to 30 minutes, until lightly browned. Remove from the oven and let the rolls cool slightly on the baking sheets for about 5 minutes. Raise the oven heat to 375°F.

7. Transfer each roll to a cutting board and slice each roll on the diagonal into 3/4-inch-thick slices. Lay the slices on the cookie sheets, cut side up, and bake for about 5 minutes, until lightly browned and crisp around the edges. Cool completely on wire racks. Store in an airtight container.

Postre del Sol

This recipe is a Ranch favorite. When strawberries or peaches are in season, I love to use them in fruit butters. These cookies are formed in brioche cups and so when baked and filled, they resemble little suns—thus the name, which means "pastry of the sun!"

COOKIES

3/4 cup packed light or dark brown sugar
3/8 cup canola oil margarine
2 large egg whites
2 1/2 cups whole wheat flour

FILLING

1 cup part-skim ricotta cheese
1 teaspoon dark or light brown sugar
Pinch of ground cinnamon
1/2 teaspoon vanilla extract
Fruit Butter (page 8)
25 fresh mint leaves

1. Preheat the oven to 350°F. Lightly spray 10 to 12 (or more) fluted brioche or cookie molds with vegetable oil spray. Set the molds on a cookie sheet.

2. To make the cookies, in the bowl of an electric mixer set on medium-high speed, combine the brown sugar and the margarine and beat until smooth and creamy. Add the egg whites and beat until well blended. Add the flour and blend on medium-low speed until incorporated. Don't overmix.

Per Cookie
(not including
Fruit Butter):
97 calories
4 g total fat (33% of calories)
1 g saturated fat
3 mg cholesterol
3 g protein (13% of calories)
14 g carbohydrates (54% of calories)
2 g fiber
51 mg sodium
Makes 25

DESSERTS

3. With floured hands, pinch off small balls about the size of a large walnut (approximately 2 tablespoons). Press the dough balls into the brioche molds. Bake for 15 to 20 minutes or until the cookies are golden brown. (Take care not to burn.) Gently unmold the cookies and cool on wire racks. Let the molds cool before baking the next batch of cookies, spraying them again, if necessary, with vegetable oil spray.

4. To make the filling, in a medium bowl, combine the ricotta, brown sugar, cinnamon, and vanilla and whisk until smooth and well mixed. Spoon into a pastry bag fitted with a star tip and pipe a 1/2 teaspoon-size star into the center of each cookie.

5. Gently spoon about 2 tablespoons of Fruit Butter around each star and serve.

NOTE: *Brioche molds are available at cookware shops. Unfilled, the cookie crusts can be stored in an airtight container for up to 1 month, or they can be frozen for up to 3 months if well wrapped and place in a sealed container.*

Taking the Ranch Home

What to do in the time you set aside? Professor Szekely used to say, "Moderation in everything—even in moderation!" A recurring theme at Rancho La Puerta is balance, whether it's a rediscovery of the muscles needed to stand on one foot during a yoga pose or the balance of mind, body, and spirit in a too-harried world of work, family commitments, and the very little time one has to eat properly and enjoyably. Seek balance. Exercise in a way that you *enjoy,* and you'll use up calories while positively recharging your batteries instead of wearing them down. Grimly pounding the floor in an uninspiring workout is not a path to true fitness.

Peach Trifle

When peaches are in season, the Ranch guests crave this delightful dessert. Trifle is traditionally a pound cake awash in Chantilly cream, rich custard, sherry, and raspberry jam. Ours, obviously, has a fraction of the fat. Any fruit will work here, so use a favorite in other seasons.

3 peaches, peeled, pitted, and coarsely chopped
1/2 cup nonfat ricotta cheese
1/2 cup plain nonfat yogurt
1 tablespoon fresh lime juice
1 teaspoon ground cinnamon
1 teaspoon vanilla extract
3 tablespoons brown sugar, or to taste (optional)
1/4 cup Rancho La Puerta Granola (page 3)
3 tablespoons Nonfat Chocolate Sauce (page 250)

1. In a blender or food processor, combine the peaches, ricotta, yogurt, lime juice, cinnamon, and vanilla and process until blended. Taste, and add the brown sugar, if using. Process again just until smooth. Take care not to overprocess or the mixture might break or liquefy.

2. Spoon the mixture into a pastry bag fitted with a #9 star tip and pipe about 1/4 cup of the mixture into 6 ramekins or custard cups. Freeze for at least 2 hours and serve garnished with granola and chocolate sauce.

Per Serving:

120 calories

1 g total fat (11% of calories)

0 g saturated fat

3 mg cholesterol

5 g protein (17% of calories)

21 g carbohydrates (72% of calories)

1 g fiber

26 mg sodium

Makes 6 servings

NOTE: *Alternatively, spoon the mixture into an ice cream maker and freeze according to the manufacturer's instructions. Serve spooned into ramekins or small dessert bowls.*

Apple Strudel with Raspberries

I use Granny Smith apples because they're tart and don't soften when baked.

STRUDEL

6 Granny Smith or other tart apples, peeled, seeded, and sliced
1 tablespoon fresh lime juice
1 tablespoon light or dark brown sugar
1/2 teaspoon ground cinnamon
1/2 teaspoon ground ginger
1/4 cup raisins
6 sheets phyllo dough, about 14 by 18 inches
1/2 cup fresh or dried bread crumbs (see Note)

TOPPING

1 tablespoon ground cinnamon
1 tablespoon light or dark brown sugar

SAUCE AND GARNISH:

1 1/2 cups Raspberry Sauce (page 246)
1 1/2 cups fresh raspberries
6 sprigs fresh mint

Per Serving:

232 calories

2 g total fat (9% of calories)

0 g saturated fat

0 mg cholesterol

5 g protein (7% of calories)

51 g carbohydrates (84% of calories)

8 g fiber

172 mg sodium

Makes 6 servings

1. Preheat the oven to 375°F. Line a baking sheet or sheet pan with parchment paper and lightly spray the paper with vegetable oil spray and set aside.

2. To make the strudel, in a large bowl, combine the apples, lime juice, brown sugar, cinnamon, ginger, and raisins and toss to mix.

3. Lightly spray a large sauté pan with vegetable oil spray. Transfer the apple mixture to the pan and cook over medium-high heat for about 5 minutes, until the apples begin to soften. Remove from the heat, drain, and set aside to cool slightly.

4. Lay a clean dish towel on a dry work surface and smooth a sheet of phyllo dough. Spray lightly with vegetable oil spray and sprinkle 1 tablespoon of bread crumbs over the dough. Top with another sheet of phyllo, spray with vegetable oil spray, and sprinkle on more bread crumbs. Continue until all 6 sheets are stacked.

5. Spread the cooled apple mixture on the stack of phyllo and fold approximately 2 inches of each narrow end over the filling to contain it during rolling. Using the dish towel as a guide, gently roll the strudel into a cylinder, beginning with the long end facing you. The cylinder will be about 14 inches long. Transfer, seam side down, to the prepared baking sheet. Lightly spray the strudel with vegetable oil spray.

6. To make the topping, mix the cinnamon and brown sugar in a bowl. Sprinkle evenly over the top of the strudel and bake for about 30 minutes, until golden brown. Remove from the oven to cool slightly on the pan. While still warm, but not hot, transfer the strudel to a wire rack to cool completely.

7. When completely cool, slice into 6 equal portions and spoon the sauce over each serving. Garnish with raspberries and mint.

NOTE: *Fresh bread crumbs are easily made by processing bread in a blender or food processor. One slice of commercial bread yields about 1/2 cup of crumbs. Any sort of stale bread makes good crumbs and these are generally preferable to store-bought crumbs. If using dried, commercially packaged crumbs, be sure to use plain, unseasoned crumbs.*

Blueberry Cheesecake

As a little boy I remember eating one of my grandmother's fresh blueberry pies all by myself. I ate it slowly—it was steaming hot—and I washed it down with several glasses of milk. I still love blueberries, and I use their extraordinary color and fresh taste in this low-fat cheesecake.

CRUMB CRUST
1 1/3 cups fine graham cracker crumbs (about 11 whole graham crackers)
1/4 cup unsweetened, unfiltered apple juice

FILLING
1/3 cup unsweetened, unfiltered apple juice
1 tablespoon (1 envelope) unflavored gelatin
11/2 cups plain nonfat yogurt
1/2 cup nonfat ricotta cheese
1/4 cup packed light or dark brown sugar, or to taste
2 tablespoons fresh lime juice
1 cup fresh blueberries

GARNISH
10 fresh blueberries
10 sprigs fresh mint

1. Preheat the oven to 350°F. Lightly spray a 9-inch pie pan with vegetable oil spray.

2. To make the crust, put the crumbs in a small bowl, add the apple juice, and stir with a fork until the crumbs are moist but not sticky. Press the crumb mixture onto the pie pan, pressing it up the sides and bottom of the pan. Bake for about 15 minutes or until golden, taking care not to let it burn. (Cracks in the crust are normal in oil-free crusts.) Set the crust on a wire rack to cool completely.

Per Serving:

119 calories

2 g total fat (18% of calories)

1 g saturated fat

4 mg cholesterol

4 g protein (14% of calories)

21 g carbohydrates (68% of calories)

1 g fiber

121 mg sodium

Makes 10 servings

3. To make the filling, in a small saucepan, bring the apple juice to a simmer over medium heat. Turn off the heat but leave the saucepan on the burner. Sprinkle the gelatin over the juice and stir until the gelatin dissolves.

4. In a food processor or blender, combine the yogurt, ricotta cheese, brown sugar, lime juice, and gelatin mixture and process until smooth. Scrape into a bowl and fold in 3/4 cup of blueberries. Taste and adjust the sweetness with brown sugar. Pour into the cooled crust and smooth with a spatula.

5. In a food processor or blender, puree the remaining 1/4 cup of blueberries until smooth. Strain through a fine sieve, pressing against the berries to extract as much juice as possible. Pour into a clean squeeze bottle and squirt thin parallel lines on top of the filling. Rotate the pie 90° and using a toothpick or knife point, intersect each blueberry line to make a wavy pattern. Refrigerate for at least 2 hours.

6. To serve, cut into 10 portions and garnish with a drizzle of puree on the corner of each serving. Top each piece with a blueberry and a mint sprig.

NOTE: *To make the graham cracker crumbs, process the whole crackers in a food processor until finely ground.*

If the gelatin thickens before it is added to the filling, reheat it. Cold liquid makes the gelatin lump; boiling it causes it to loose some of its gelling power.

Orange-Lime Cheesecake

Here's a great low-fat cheesecake. You'll like this one—but who wouldn't?

Per Serving:

113 calories

2 g total fat (18% of calories)

1 g saturated fat

4 mg cholesterol

4 g protein (15% of calories)

19 g carbohydrates (67% of calories)

1 g fiber

120 mg sodium

Makes 10 servings

CRUMB CRUST

1 1/3 cups fine graham cracker crumbs (about 11 whole graham crackers)

1/4 cup unsweetened, unfiltered apple juice

FILLING

1/3 cup unsweetened unfiltered apple juice

1 tablespoon (1 envelope) unflavored gelatin

1 1/2 cups plain nonfat yogurt

1/2 cup nonfat ricotta cheese

1/4 cup packed light or dark brown sugar, or to taste

2 tablespoons fresh orange juice

2 tablespoons fresh lime juice

2 tablespoons grated lime zest

1 tablespoon grated orange zest

GARNISH

1 orange, peeled and cut into 1/8-inch-thick slices

10 sprigs fresh mint

1. Preheat the oven to 350°F. Lightly spray a 9-inch pie pan with vegetable oil spray.

2. To make the crust, put the crumbs in a small bowl, add the apple juice, and stir with a fork until the crumbs are moist but not sticky. Press the crumb mixture onto the pie pan, pressing it up the sides and bottom of the pan. Bake for about 15 minutes or until golden, taking care not to let it burn. (Cracks in the crust are normal in oil-free crusts.) Set the crust on a wire rack to cool completely.

3. To make the filling, in a small saucepan, bring the apple juice to a simmer over medium heat. Turn off the heat but leave the saucepan on the burner. Sprinkle the gelatin over the juice and stir until the gelatin dissolves.

4. In a food processor or blender, combine the yogurt, ricotta cheese, brown sugar, juices, zests, and the gelatin mixture and process until smooth. Taste and adjust the sweetness with brown sugar. Pour into the cooled crust and smooth with a spatula. Refrigerate for at least 2 hours.

5. To serve, cut into 10 portions and garnish each with an orange slice and a mint sprig.

Sweet Potato Pie

Actually, I prefer using what most folks think of as red yams instead of smaller, drier sweet potatoes in these pies because they have a creamier consistency and richer taste, but the title "Red Yam Pie" doesn't have quite the right ring to it I want. You can also substitute yams from the Red Yams with Oranges (page 200).

CRUMB CRUST

1 1/3 cups fine graham cracker crumbs (about 11 whole graham crackers)

1/4 cup unsweetened, unfiltered apple juice

FILLING

2 sweet potatoes, peeled and cut into 1-inch cubes

1 cup fresh orange juice

Grated zest of 1 orange

1 teaspoon ground cinnamon

2 teaspoons vanilla extract

1 banana (optional)

1/2 cup nonfat ricotta cheese

4 large egg whites

1/4 cup honey

1/4 teaspoon ground nutmeg

1/4 teaspoon ground cloves

TOPPING (OPTIONAL)

1/4 cup part-skim ricotta cheese

2 teaspoons maple syrup

1/4 teaspoon vanilla extract

1/4 teaspoon grated orange zest

Per Serving (without topping):

160 calories

3 g total fat (14% of calories)

1 g saturated fat

4 g cholesterol

5 g protein (11% of calories)

31 g carbohydrates (75% of calories)

2 g fiber

118 mg sodium

Makes 10 servings

1. Preheat the oven to 350°F. Lightly spray a 9-inch pie pan with vegetable oil spray.

2. To make the crust, put the crumbs in a small bowl, add the apple juice, and stir with a fork until the crumbs are moist but not sticky. Press the crumb mixture onto the pie pan, pressing it up the sides and bottom of the pan. Bake for about 15 minutes or until golden, taking care not to let it burn. (Cracks in the crust are normal in oil-free crusts.) Set the crust on a wire rack to cool. Do not turn the oven off.

3. To make the filling, in a large saucepan, combine the sweet potatoes, juice, zest, 1/2 teaspoon cinnamon, and 1 teaspoon vanilla and add enough cold water just to cover the potatoes. Bring to a boil over high heat, reduce the heat, and simmer, uncovered, for about 30 minutes, until the potatoes are fork-tender. Drain and transfer the potatoes to a food processor and process until smooth. (You will have about 2 cups of puree; you may be able to mash the potatoes with a fork instead.)

4. Add the banana, ricotta, egg whites, and honey to the potatoes and pulse to mix. Season with the remaining 1/2 teaspoon cinnamon, the nutmeg, cloves, and remaining 1 teaspoon vanilla and process until smooth.

5. Scrape the filling into the crust and smooth the top. Bake on the center rack of the oven for about 40 minutes, or until the filling is firm. If the crust starts to burn during baking, lay strips of aluminum foil over the edges. Cool on a wire rack and when room temperature, refrigerate for at least 2 hours, until chilled.

6. To make the topping, in a food processor, combine the ricotta, maple syrup, vanilla, and zest and process until smooth.

7. Serve the pie cut into wedges and garnished with dollops of ricotta topping, if desired.

NOTE: *A 15-ounce can of drained sweet potatoes can be substituted for fresh. You can also substitute cooked pumpkin or summer squash or canned unsweetened pumpkin puree.*

Corn Crepes with Strawberry Sauce

Any seasonal fruit, such as peaches, nectarines, apricots, blueberries, raspberries, and apples, can be substituted for the strawberries.

CREPES

2/3 cup whole wheat pastry flour

1/3 cup stone-ground yellow cornmeal

1/4 teaspoon ground cinnamon

1/4 teaspoon ground cardamom

1/4 teaspoon ground nutmeg

4 large egg whites

2 cups skim milk

1 tablespoon honey

1/4 teaspoon vanilla extract

SAUCE

2 cups hulled and sliced strawberries

1/2 cup unfiltered, unsweetened apple juice

3 tablespoons fresh lime juice

Fructose (optional)

1. To make the crepes, in a large bowl, combine the flour, cornmeal, cinnamon, cardamom, and nutmeg and whisk well to mix.

2. In a small bowl, whisk the egg whites until frothy. Add the milk, honey, and vanilla and whisk to mix.

Per Serving:

149 calories

1 g total fat (4% of calories)

0 g saturated fat

1 mg cholesterol

7 g protein (18% of calories)

30 g carbohydrates (78% of calories)

3 g fiber

60 mg sodium

Makes 6 servings

3. Pour the wet ingredients into dry ingredients and stir with a wooden spoon just until combined. Take care not to overmix or the pancakes will be tough. Cover and refrigerate the batter for at least 30 minutes.

4. To prepare the sauce, in a saucepan, combine the strawberries, apple juice, and lime juice and simmer over medium heat for 8 to 10 minutes, until the berries soften. Sweeten to taste with fructose, if necessary, and set aside.

5. Spray a griddle or nonstick sauté pan with vegetable oil spray and heat over medium heat. Using a small ladle, spoon about 3 tablespoons of batter onto the griddle for each crepe and cook until the bubbles that form on the top of the crepe break apart and the bottom is golden. Turn and cook the other side for several seconds until set. Continue until all the batter is used.

6. Immediately transfer the crepes once cooked to serving plates and spoon the fruit sauce over them.

NOTE: *The crepes can be made ahead of time, wrapped well in plastic wrap, and frozen. When ready to use, heat them in the microwave or in a hot, dry sauté pan or griddle.*

Cinnamon Flan

To add beauty and enrich the flavor of this classic dish, prepare the caramel topping for these little flans. The caramel will add 30 calories per serving but no fat. With or without the caramel, these are a treat!

1/3 cup packed light brown sugar, for topping (optional)
1 quart 1% low-fat milk
1/4 cup packed dark or light brown sugar
1/2 teaspoon ground cinnamon
1 vanilla bean, split lengthwise, or 2 teaspoons vanilla extract
8 large egg whites
1 large egg yolk
8 cinnamon sticks
8 sprigs fresh mint

1. If making the topping, heat the brown sugar in a sauté pan set over low heat for a 2 or 3 minutes, until the sugar melts. Raise the heat and using a dry wooden spoon, stir until the sugar is very hot and looks medium brown in color (take care the sugar does not burn). Spoon equal amounts of melted sugar into eight 4-ounce ramekins or custard cups and set aside to cool completely.

2. In a saucepan or the top of a double boiler set over simmering water, combine the milk, brown sugar, cinnamon, and vanilla bean and cook over medium heat for about 15 minutes, stirring constantly, until smooth. Set aside to cool. Remove and discard the vanilla bean or save it for another use.

Per Serving (without topping):

126 calories
2 g total fat (15% of calories)
1 g saturated fat
31 g cholesterol
8 g protein (25% of calories)
19 g carbohydrates (60% of calories)
1 g fiber
122 mg sodium

Makes 8 servings

DESSERTS

3. Preheat the oven to 350°F.

4. In a bowl, whisk the egg whites and yolk until frothy. Stir into the cooled milk mixture. Pour into ramekins, filling each about three-fourths full, and set the ramekins in a roasting pan. Pour hot water into the pan until it comes about halfway up the sides of the ramekins. Cover the pan with aluminum foil (this will prevent skin forming on the custard) and bake on the lowest rack of the oven for about 1 hour, or until set and a toothpick or sharp knife inserted in the center of a custard comes out clean. Let the custards cool in the water bath and then refrigerate for at least 2 hours.

5. Unmold each flan by lightly pressing around the edge of each flan to break the seal. Invert onto a dessert plate and garnish with cinnamon sticks and mint sprigs.

Mango-Orange Sorbet

The method used here is only one of several ways to make sorbet. Another way is to freeze the fruit first, puree it in a food processor, and add the juice while the motor is running. Store this mixture in containers in the freezer.

2 large mangoes (about 8 ounces each), pitted and peeled
1 cup fresh orange juice
1 banana, cut into large pieces
2 to 3 tablespoons fresh lime juice
1 kiwi, peeled and sliced
6 sprigs fresh mint

1. In a food processor, combine the mango, orange juice, banana, lime juice, and kiwi and process until smooth. Pour into an 8-inch square freezer-proof dish and freeze for at least 2 hours.

2. Scrape the mixture back into the food processor and mix until smooth and fluffy. Return to the dish and freeze an additional 2 hours.

3. Chill dessert dishes for about 20 minutes in the freezer before serving. Scoop the sorbet onto the dishes, garnished mint sprigs.

Per Serving:
99 calories
0 g total fat (4% of calories)
0 g saturated fat
0 mg cholesterol
1 g protein (4% of calories)
23 g carbohydrates (92% of calories)
1 g fiber
3 mg sodium
Makes 6 servings

Strawberry-Banana Sorbet

When bananas and strawberries are ripe, freeze them (peel the bananas first) in heavy-duty plastic bags or containers for up to a month. The bananas may darken a little, but if well wrapped they won't turn black and their flavor will be sweet and wonderful.

1 banana, peeled and frozen
1 cup frozen stemmed and thickly sliced strawberries
1 cup fresh orange juice or juice of choice

1. In a food processor, combine the banana, frozen strawberries, and juice and process until smooth. Pour into an 8-inch square freezer-proof dish and freeze for at least 2 hours.

2. Scrape the mixture back into the food processor and mix until smooth and fluffy. Return to the dish and freeze an additional 2 hours.

3. Chill dessert dishes for about 20 minutes in the freezer before serving. Scoop the sorbet onto the dishes, garnished mint sprigs.

Per Serving:

65 calories

0 g total fat (5% of calories)

0 g saturated fat

0 mg cholesterol

1 g protein (6% of calories)

16 g carbohydrates (89% of calories)

2 g fiber

1 mg sodium

Makes 4 servings

Frozen Strawberry Yogurt

Substitute nearly any fruit, such as bananas, peaches, mangoes, or pineapple, for the strawberries. If you don't mind adding about 30 calories per serving, sprinkle a teaspoon of Rancho La Puerta Granola (page 3) on the yogurt. Yum!

1 cup hulled and sliced fresh strawberries
1 cup nonfat plain yogurt
1 teaspoon vanilla extract
1/2 teaspoon ground cinnamon
2 teaspoons fructose, or to taste (optional)

1. In a blender or food processor, combine the strawberries, yogurt, vanilla, and cinnamon and process until smooth. Taste and sweeten with fructose, if desired.

2. Transfer to an ice cream maker and freeze according to the manufacturer's directions.

Per Serving:
56 calories
0 g total fat (4% of calories)
0 g saturated fat
1 mg cholesterol
3 g protein (25% of calories)
10 g carbohydrates (71% of calories)
0 g fiber
44 mg sodium
Makes 4 servings

Taking the Ranch Home

The optimum time to exercise? Whenever you'll do it! Many guests at the ranch find themselves rising with the dawn's first light to hike and stretch, long before breakfast. The fresh air and the absence of a business calendar brings out the early bird in most. But once you return home, be assured that if you're a night person and someone says you must get up at 5:30 A.M. to exercise, forget it; the plan will probably fail. If it takes discipline, you'll weary of it. Find friends to exercise with. As happens at the ranch, you'll experience yourself saying, "So, see you tomorrow morning for another walk?"

Grilled Pineapple

Grilling intensifies the pineapple's flavor. Make this dessert after the rest of the meal has been grilled and the coals are still hot.

1 cup fresh orange juice
2 tablespoons coarsely chopped dried prunes
1 tablespoon raisins
1 tablespoon dried cranberries
1/4 teaspoon vanilla extract
1/4 teaspoon ground cinnamon
Six 1/2-inch-thick pineapple rings

1. Prepare a charcoal or gas grill so that the coals are medium-hot.

2. In a small saucepan, combine the orange juice, prunes, raisins, cranberries, vanilla, and cinnamon and stir gently to combine. Add the pineapple rings and set aside for about 15 minutes to macerate the fruit.

3. Bring the mixture to a simmer over low heat and cook for 2 to 3 minutes. Remove from the heat and lift the pineapple from the pan. Cover the pan to keep the sauce warm.

4. Grill the pineapple rings for about 1 minute on each side, until nicely marked with grill marks. Set each in the center of a dessert plate and spoon sauce over them.

Per Serving:
186 calories
0 g total fat (1% of calories)
0 g saturated fat
0 mg cholesterol
2 g protein (96% of calories)
48 g carbohydrates (3% of calories)
2 g fiber
3 mg sodium
Makes 6 servings

Baked Mexican Bananas with Cinnamon

Serve these over frozen yogurt.

3 bananas, quartered horizontally
1/2 teaspoon grated orange zest
1/4 teaspoon grated lime zest
1/2 cup fresh orange juice
1 teaspoon fresh lime juice
1/4 cup raisins or currants
1/4 teaspoon vanilla extract
1/4 teaspoon ground cinnamon

Per Serving:
120 calories
0 g total fat (3% of calories)
0 g saturated fat
0 mg cholesterol
1 g protein (4% of calories)
28 g carbohydrates (92% of calories)
1 g fiber
2 mg sodium
Makes 4 servings

1. Preheat the oven to 375°F.

2. In a shallow baking dish just large enough to hold them, arrange the bananas in a single layer.

3. In a small bowl, combine the zests, juices, currants, vanilla, and cinnamon and whisk to blend. Pour over the bananas and bake, uncovered, for about 20 minutes or until the bananas are lightly browned and bubbling.

4. Use a spatula to put 3 banana pieces in the center of each plate and spoon the sauce from the dish over them.

Raspberry Sauce

This delicious low-fat topping can be used with most desserts or fruit plates. You can substitute other berries, bananas, kiwis, mangoes, peaches, papayas, or whatever other fruit you like for the raspberries—just be sure it can be pureed in a food processor. Apples, pears, and quinces are hard and require poaching to soften them up before pureeing. Some of my friends drink this as a smoothie.

1 cup raspberries
1/4 cup nonfat plain yogurt
1 teaspoon chopped fresh mint leaves
1/2 teaspoon fresh lime juice
1/2 teaspoon light brown sugar, or to taste

In a blender or food processor, combine the raspberries, yogurt, mint, and lime juice and process until smooth. Taste and adjust the sweetness with the sugar. Process again and serve immediately.

Per Serving:
16 calories
0 g fat (7% of calories)
0 g saturated fat
0 mg cholesterol
1 g protein (17% of calories)
3 g carbohydrates (76% of calories)
1 g fiber
7 mg sodium
Makes 6 servings

Raspberry-Strawberry Sauce

During strawberry season, this is a favorite with our guests.

1 cup hulled strawberries
1/2 cup raspberries
1 banana, chopped
1 tablespoon fresh orange juice
1/2 teaspoon vanilla extract
1/4 teaspoon ground cinnamon

In a food processor or blender, combine all the ingredients and process until smooth. Serve immediately.

Per Serving:

25 calories

0 g total fat (6% of calories)

0 g saturated fat

0 mg cholesterol

0 g protein (5% of calories)

6 g carbohydrates (88% of calories)

0 g fiber

0 mg sodium

Makes 8 servings

Banana Sauce

Great over fruit salads and desserts, or as a smoothie. I use very ripe bananas so that extra sugar or honey isn't necessary.

2 bananas, chopped
1 tablespoon fresh orange juice
1 tablespoon fresh lime juice
1/2 teaspoon vanilla extract
1/4 teaspoon ground cinnamon

Place all of the ingredients in a blender or food processor and process until smooth.

Per Serving:
28 calories
0 g total fat (4% of calories)
0 g saturated fat
0 mg cholesterol
0 g protein (4% of calories)
6 g carbohydrates (92% of calories)
0 g fiber
0 mg sodium
Makes 8 servings

Guava Sauce

Guavas are a tropical fruit with a sweet-and-sour citrus flavor. This sauce goes well with fruit salad, spooned over sorbets, pastries, or even on toast. Use very ripe bananas and guavas because the fruit will be exceptionally sweet, but add a little sugar or honey if needed.

1 cup chopped guavas (about 5 ounces total)
1/2 banana
1 teaspoon fresh lime juice
1/2 teaspoon vanilla extract
1/4 teaspoon ground cinnamon

In a food processor or blender, combine the ingredients and process until smooth. Transfer to a fine sieve and strain into a bowl by pushing on the fruit with the back of a spoon—guavas have many small seeds that need to be strained. Serve immediately or cover and refrigerate for up to 2 days.

Per Serving:
17 calories
0 g total fat (7% of calories)
0 g saturated fat
0 mg cholesterol
0 g protein (5% of calories)
4 g carbohydrates (88% of calories)
1 g fiber
1 mg sodium
Makes 8 servings

Nonfat Chocolate Sauce

Serve this chocolate sauce over fresh fruit, a frozen dessert, or a slice of bread. It will satisfy your most intense chocolate craving.

1/2 cup skim milk

1 tablespoon strong brewed coffee (see Note)

1/2 teaspoon cornstarch

1/4 cup unsweetened cocoa powder

1/4 cup brown sugar

In a small saucepan, combine the milk, coffee, and cornstarch and stir until the cornstarch dissolves. Stir in the cocoa and brown sugar and bring to a simmer over medium heat. Cook for about 5 minutes, stirring, until the sauce thickens and is no longer cloudy. Set aside to cool. Use when cool or cover and refrigerate for up to 2 days.

Per Serving:

31 calories

0 g total fat (11% of calories)

0 g saturated fat

0 mg cholesterol

1 g protein (13% of calories)

6 g carbohydrates (76% of calories)

0 g fiber

28 mg sodium

Makes 8 servings

NOTE: *If you do not have any brewed coffee, dissolve 1 teaspoon of freeze-dried decaffeinated coffee granules in 1 tablespoon of water.*

Bill's Spa Birthday Cake

Every week, we have about 150 guests at the Ranch and so it's not surprising that we celebrate lots of birthdays. This is the low-fat cake I bake to mark these occasions and it's always a big hit. I get asked for the recipe over and over. I add cornstarch to the batter to lighten the texture, and carrots and bananas for moisture and sweetness. The Spa Frosting is a bonus. You could opt to serve the cake with a dusting of confectioners' sugar and fresh sliced fruit, if you prefer.

1 cup cake flour

3/8 cup whole wheat flour

2 tablespoons cornstarch

1 tablespoon cinnamon

1 1/4 teaspoons baking powder

1/2 teaspoon baking soda

1 cup skim milk

1/2 cup lightly packed light brown sugar

1 1/4 cups mashed banana (2 1/2 bananas, about 6 ounces)

1 tablespoon canola oil

1 teaspoon pure vanilla extract

1/2 cup shredded carrots

3 large egg whites, at room temperature

1/4 teaspoon cream of tartar

Per Serving (without frosting):

124 calories

0 g total fat (12% of calories)

0 g saturated fat

0 mg cholesterol

4 g protein (11% of calories)

24 g carbohydrates (77% of calories)

1 g fiber

143 mg sodium

Makes 10 servings

1. Preheat the oven to 350°F. Lightly spray two 9-inch round cake pans with vegetable oil spray. Line the bottom of the pans with parchment paper or wax paper. Lightly spray the paper. Alternatively, bake the cake in a single layer in a 15 by 10-inch jelly roll pan.

2. In a bowl, mix together the flours, cornstarch, cinnamon, baking powder, and baking soda and whisk 7 or 8 times. Set aside.

3. In a mixing bowl, combine the milk, brown sugar, 1/4 cup of the banana, oil, and vanilla and stir with a spatula or wooden spoon. Add the carrots and mix well. Fold in the dry ingredients just until incorporated. Do not over mix.

4. In a separate clean, dry bowl, using an electric mixer set on medium

speed, beat the egg whites and cream of tartar for about 1 minute until foamy. Raise the speed to high and beat until soft peaks form. To test for this, lift the beaters; the whites should peak but the peak will fall over. Gently fold the whites into the batter just until incorporated. It is acceptable if a few specks of white remain in the batter.

5. Scrape the batter into the prepared pan and smooth the top. Bake on the center rack of the oven for 40 to 45 minutes or until a toothpick inserted in the center of the cake comes out clean and the edges begin to pull away from the sides of the pan. Let the cake cool in the pan set on a wire rack for about 5 minutes. Turn the cake layers out onto wire racks, peel off the paper and let cool completely.

6. Using a serrated knife, split the cake layers horizontally into 4 thin layers. Spread the remaining 1/2 cup of mashed banana between the layers and stack them. Frost the top and sides of the cake with Spa Frosting (page 253). For a sheet cake, do not split into layers. Simply frost the top.

Spa Frosting

1 cup skim ricotta cheese

1/2 cup silken tofu

2 tablespoons lightly packed light brown sugar

1 teaspoon pure vanilla extract

In a mixing bowl, combine the milk and tofu and whisk until smooth. Add the sugar and vanilla and blend until smooth and a good consistency for spreading. Use immediately.

Per Tablespoon:

19 calories

1 g total fat (45% of calories)

1 g saturated fat

3 mg cholesterol

1 g protein (30% of calories)

1 g carbohydrates (25% of calories)

0 g fiber

12 mg sodium

Makes 28 servings

Beverages

ALL OF US KNOW *that we must replenish thirsty bodies with drink. Without water from its ancient aquifer, Rancho La Puerta would be very dry indeed. The Ranch is abundant with native plant life that depends only on our scant rainfall, but we rely on irrigation to grow the tender vegetables we need for our tables.*

So irrigate that body of yours. Sip herbal tea or enjoy a cool, crisp limeade. Guests are given their own water bottles upon arrival to assure that they'll never be without water. They refill often, and I do, too, in the kitchen—at least eight big glasses a day.

Calientito—Little Hot One

On cooler winter days at the Ranch we mix up Calientito, meaning "little hot one"—a spiced drink brewed with little pieces of chopped fruit. There are as many flavors of Calientitos as there are fruit, but one of my favorites is guava, apple, and raisins seasoned with cinnamon and vanilla.

1 quart unsweetened, unfiltered apple juice

1 apple, cored and chopped

1 orange, sliced

1 pear, cored and chopped

2 cups hulled strawberries

1/2 cup chopped pineapple

1 heaping tablespoon raisins (15 to 20 raisins)

2 to 3 cinnamon sticks

2 whole cloves

1 tablespoon vanilla extract

In a large saucepan, combine all the ingredients and simmer over medium heat. Simmer for 15 to 20 minutes, then serve immediately.

Per Serving:

59 calories

1 g total fat (8% of calories)

0 g saturated fat

0 mg cholesterol

1 g protein (5% of calories)

13 g carbohydrates (87% of calories)

1 g fiber

9 mg sodium

Makes 8 servings

Almond-Banana Milk

This refreshing drink is quick to make and acts as a great pick-me-up or energy booster. Give it a try.

2 cups unsweetened, unfiltered apple juice
2 tablespoons coarsely chopped almonds
1 banana, sliced
1 cup ice cubes

In a food processor or blender, combine all the ingredients and process until nearly smooth. Serve at once.

Per Serving:

111 calories

3 g total fat (20% of calories)

0 g saturated fat

0 mg cholesterol

1 g protein (4% of calories)

22 g carbohydrates (76% of calories)

1 g fiber

6 mg sodium

Makes 4 servings

Taking the Ranch Home

Go tell it on the mountain . . . Any walk by yourself has great value. We need those moments alone with our thoughts. But a walk with friends adds a shared social experience to any workout. On the ranch's mountain hikes, new friendships are made every morning before 8:30 A.M., yet the same chatting hikers also fall silent as they listen to their breathing on a hilly stretch or hear the trilling *tink-tink-tink-tink* of a dusky California towhee in the chaparral. Out in nature, greeting the sun, talking with friends about days past and days to come, for once the cliché holds true—it's the best of both worlds.

Strawberry-Banana Smoothie

Substitute any favorite fruit for the strawberries; and use mango, orange, or grape juice in place of apple juice. Experiment and enjoy.

4 cups hulled strawberries
2 bananas
1 cup unsweetened, unfiltered apple juice
2 to 3 tablespoons fresh lime juice
1/2 cup ice cubes
Mint leaves, for garnish

In a blender, combine the ingredients and process until smooth. Pour into glasses, garnish with mint leaves, and serve immediately.

Per Serving:

102 calories

1 g total fat (7% of calories)

0 g saturated fat

0 mg cholesterol

1 g protein (6% of calories)

22 g carbohydrates (87% of calories)

1 g fiber

7 mg sodium

Makes 4 servings

NOTE: *I don't recommend substituting pineapple for any of the fruit in this recipe because it is so high in fiber.*

Limeade Tecate Style

Most of the year—and especially in the summertime here in the high desert of northern Baja—I make fresh iced limeade with plump green Mexican limes, or limas, *as they are called in Mexico. It's just what the doctor ordered after a day filled with exercise and fresh air. When limes are plentiful in your market, pick some up and give this a try.*

8 fresh limes, juiced
Light brown sugar, to taste (optional)

In a large pitcher, combine 4 cups water and the lime juice. Add sugar to taste, if desired, stirring until dissolved. Serve over ice.

Per Serving:
65 calories
0 g total fat (3% of calories)
0 g saturated fat
0 mg cholesterol
1 g protein (5% of calories)
21 g carbohydrates (92% of calories)
5 g fiber
12 mg sodium
Makes 4 servings

Livia's Lemon Verbena and Rose Hip Tea

Livia is Deborah Szekely's daughter and the architectural designer for *Tres Estrellas*, our wonderful organic garden where we grow so much of our food. By designing this garden, Livia realized her father Edmond's dream of eating from a totally organic garden. Her efforts, plus those of skilled local gardeners, have made the Ranch's gardens among the most beautiful on earth.

This refreshing tea is made with herbs from the garden. You can steep these separately because they are both flavorful, or you can combine them. Lemon verbena is a long, narrow leaf full of lemony flavor and so refreshing. Rose hips provide a floral citrus flavor and are an excellent source of vitamin C. You can pick these up at your local health food store or in your own garden.

1/2 cup torn lemon verbena leaves
1/4 cup rose hips
Honey, to taste

1. Place 4 cups water in a tea kettle or medium saucepan and bring to a boil over medium-high heat. Reduce the heat to a simmer and add the leaves and rose hips. Remove from the heat and steep for about 15 minutes.

2. Return to the heat and simmer for 1 minute. Pour into individual tea cups or mugs, sweeten with honey if desired, and serve.

Per Serving:

16 calories

0 g total fat (3% of calories)

0 g saturated fat

0 mg cholesterol

1 g protein (14% of calories)

4 g carbohydrates (83% of calories)

0 g fiber

13 mg sodium

Makes 4 servings

Index